Charles Henry Hall

Sermons preached before the University of Oxford at St. Mary's Church

In the year MDCCXCVIII

Charles Henry Hall

Sermons preached before the University of Oxford at St. Mary's Church
In the year MDCCXCVIII

ISBN/EAN: 9783337113698

Printed in Europe, USA, Canada, Australia, Japan

Cover: Foto ©Lupo / pixelio.de

More available books at www.hansebooks.com

SERMONS

PREACHED BEFORE

THE UNIVERSITY OF OXFORD,

AT ST. MARY'S CHURCH,

IN THE YEAR MDCCXCVIII,

AT THE

LECTURE

FOUNDED BY

THE REV. JOHN BAMPTON, M. A.

BY THE

REV. CHARLES HENRY HALL, B. D.

CHAPLAIN TO THE LORD BISHOP OF EXETER,

AND

LATE STUDENT OF CHRIST CHURCH.

OXFORD:

AT THE UNIVERSITY PRESS FOR THE AUTHOR;

AND SOLD BY HANWELL AND PARKER, AND J. COOKE;
F. AND C. RIVINGTON, ST. PAUL'S CHURCH YARD,
AND HATCHARD, PICCADILLY, LONDON.

1799.

TO

THE RIGHT REVEREND FATHER IN GOD,

HENRY REGINALD,

LORD BISHOP OF EXETER,

THE

FOLLOWING DISCOURSES

ARE RESPECTFULLY INSCRIBED

BY HIS OBLIGED,

AND AFFECTIONATE SERVANT,

THE AUTHOR.

PREFACE.

It is the purpose of the following Discourses to consider at large, what is meant by the Scriptural expression, " Fulness of Time;" or, in other words, to point out the previous steps, by which God Almighty gradually prepared the way, for the introduction and promulgation of the Gospel. In such a design, there is little to awaken the attention of the learned Theologian; and, in fact, the Author has only attempted to bring under one view, and to render generally intelligible, topics and arguments, which in the writings of our best and ablest Divines have long ago been separately and thoroughly investigated.

EXTRACT

FROM THE

LAST WILL AND TESTAMENT

OF THE LATE

REV. JOHN BAMPTON,

CANON OF SALISBURY.

——" I give and bequeath my Lands
" and Eftates to the Chancellor, Mafters,
" and Scholars of the Univerfity of Ox-
" ford for ever, to have and to hold all
" fingular and the faid Lands or Eftates
" upon truft, and to the intents and pur-
" pofes hereinafter mentioned; that is to
" fay, I will and appoint that the Vice-
" Chancellor of the Univerfity of Oxford
" for

" for the time being shall take and receive
" all the rents, issues, and profits thereof,
" and (after all taxes, reparations, and ne-
" cessary deductions made) that he pay
" all the remainder to the endowment of
" eight Divinity Lecture Sermons, to be
" established for ever in the said Univer-
" sity, and to be performed in the man-
" ner following:

" I direct and appoint, that, upon the
" first Tuesday in Easter Term, a Lec-
" turer be yearly chosen by the Heads of
" Colleges only, and by no others, in the
" room adjoining to the Printing-House,
" between the hours of ten in the morn-
" ing and two in the afternoon, to preach
" eight Divinity Lecture Sermons, the year
" following, at St. Mary's in Oxford, be-
" tween the commencement of the last
" month in Lent Term, and the end of
" the third week in Act Term.

" Also I direct and appoint, that the
" eight Divinity Lecture Sermons shall be
" preached

" preached upon either of the following
" subjects—to confirm and establish the
" Christian Faith, and to confute all here-
" tics and schismatics—upon the divine
" authority of the Holy Scriptures—upon
" the authority of the writings of the
" primitive Fathers, as to the faith and
" practice of the primitive Church—upon
" the Divinity of our Lord and Saviour
" Jesus Christ—upon the Divinity of the
" Holy Ghost—upon the Articles of the
" Christian Faith, as comprehended in the
" Apostles' and Nicene Creeds.

" Also I direct, that thirty copies of the
" eight Divinity Lecture Sermons shall be
" always printed, within two months af-
" ter they are preached, and one copy
" shall be given to the Chancellor of the
" University, and one copy to the Head
" of every College, and one copy to the
" Mayor of the city of Oxford, and one
" copy to be put into the Bodleian Li-
" brary; and the expence of printing them
" shall

" shall be paid out of the revenue of the
" Land or Estates given for establishing
" the Divinity Lecture Sermons; and the
" Preacher shall not be paid, nor be en-
" titled to the revenue, before they are
" printed.

" Also I direct and appoint, that no
" person shall be qualified to preach the
" Divinity Lecture Sermons, unless he
" hath taken the Degree of Master of Arts
" at least, in one of the two Universities
" of Oxford or Cambridge; and that the
" same person shall never preach the Di-
" vinity Lecture Sermons twice."

SERMON I.

ACTS i. 7.

AND HE SAID UNTO THEM, IT IS NOT FOR YOU TO KNOW THE TIMES, OR THE SEASONS, WHICH THE FATHER HATH PUT INTO HIS OWN POWER.

SUCH was the rebuke with which our blessed Lord repressed the curiosity of his disciples, when, after he had risen from the dead, and had appeared in their assembly at Jerusalem, they eagerly enquired, whether they were at that time to look for the redemption of Israel. " Lord, wilt thou at this[a] time restore again the

[a] Acts i. 6.

kingdom to Israel?" As yet they were far from the truth; neither the works which they had seen, nor the continual appeal which they had heard to their own Prophetical Histories, had prevailed over the habitual prejudices and prepossessions, which they entertained in common with the rest of their countrymen. They expected to be the conquerors of the world; and, being accustomed, like their brethren, to indulge visionary schemes of power and dominion, until they had received the gift of the Holy Spirit, even the Apostles of our Lord seem to have formed no idea of a spiritual kingdom, or a deliverance from the slavery of sin.

A life of humiliation and a disgraceful death, were not the characters by which the Jewish nation had hoped to recognize their promised Deliverer: with expectations of a very different nature, they had framed a system of their own, calculated to sooth their national vanity, and to satisfy their lust of power: and their attachment to this fondly cherished system is of itself sufficient to account for their determined rejec-

rejection of another so directly contradictory to it—a system, which, instead of flattering their ambition by the prospect of extensive conquests, inculcated the duty of submission to their present rulers; and, far from gratifying their pride by promising them exclusive privileges as the favourites of God, avowedly declared, that every nation under heaven was to be admitted to a participation of its blessings. Had it not been for this national prepossession, which their corrupt passions and profligate morals contributed to strengthen and confirm, it is not easy to conceive how the Jews could have failed to observe the connexion between the Religion of Christ and their own Law; a connexion, which all their Prophets had taught them to expect; which our Saviour himself, at the very commencement of his ministry, expressly pointed out to them: " Think not," said he, " that I am come to destroy the Law or the Prophets: I am not come to destroy, but to fulfil [b]:" and which the Apostles afterwards explained, not to be an acci-

[b] Matt. v. 17.

dental coincidence, or a fanciful analogy, but the neceffary dependence of an imperfect preparatory law upon that which completes it.

We at this day, it is true, have many other proofs of the divine origin of our religion. We have to urge its rapid progrefs, by the miniftry of perfons to all appearance utterly incapable of producing fo extraordinary an effect, and its final eftablifhment, in defiance of the prejudices, the artifices, and the power both of the Jew and the Gentile. But we can produce no argument more forcible, or more convincing, than that which arifes from a view of the dependence of Chriftianity, not only upon the Law of Mofes, but in a more extended fenfe upon the belief and expectations of the Patriarchs, and upon every former difcovery of his will, which God had vouchfafed to make to man.

To draw this argument out at length, to view it in all its parts, and to give it all the force of which it is capable, will be the purpofe of the enfuing Lectures;—in

the

SERMON I.

the courfe of which I fhall attempt to fhew, that the whole of God's moral government of the world, and all the complicated events in the hiftory of mankind, were, in fact, nothing more than a preparation, under the guidance and control of his Providence, for the introduction of the *Chriftian Religion*; " the myftery ordained before the world [c]," " hidden from ages and generations [d]," and by the mercy of God made manifeft at laft.

God himfelf gave the firft intimation of his gracious defign: he announced to our firft parents, after their fall from a ftate of innocence, that the " feed of the woman fhould bruife the head of the ferpent [e]." To Abraham, to Ifaac, and to Jacob, he repeated the fame promife of a fpiritual deliverance, connected with the grant of worldly bleffings and temporal profperity; and, when in procefs of time the defcendants of the patriarchal family were become a flourifhing and populous nation,

[c] 1 Cor. ii. 7.   [d] Coloff. i. 26.
[e] Gen. iii. 15.

a fuca fucceffion of infpired Prophets kept alive the remembrance of the original promife, and delineated in brighter colours the nature of the deliverance to which it pointed, and the character of the perfon by whom it was to be accomplifhed.

Thus the great fcheme of Providence was gradually developed, till the "fulnefs of time arrived," in which "God, who before had fpoken at fundry times and in divers manners to the fallen race of man, thought fit at laft to fpeak to them by his Son[f]."

I am aware that there always have been, and that there ftill are, many unbelievers, who cannot difcover the wifdom of God in the progreffive communication of truth; who afk with great boldnefs, and with fome femblance perhaps of reafon, if the knowledge of Chriftianity be neceffary to the happinefs of mankind, why were fo many generations fuffered to pafs away without it? Why were its faving doctrines

[f] Heb. i. 1.

conveyed

SERMON I. 7

conveyed in dark hints, and obscure allusions? And would it not have been more consistent with the justice of God, to have revealed the truth fully and clearly at once, without the tedious and circuitous method of a preparatory dispensation?

Such objections as these, however plausible they may at first sight appear, are founded in ignorance both of the nature of man, and the ways of God; in narrow and partial views of his general Providence, and in mistaken notions of the character and design of Christianity.

Whether such a revelation as that made by Jesus Christ was, or was not, necessary, can best be determined by considering the actual state of moral and religious knowledge at the time of its promulgation. And, without entering fully into that subject at present, it may be sufficient for our purpose to ask, whether there was not in those days, upon all the great questions which involve the happiness of man, an endless variety of discordant hypotheses? Was not the providence of God, his justice,

tice, nay, his very exiftence, the theme of difpute and difcuffion in the fchools of Philofophy? Was not the immortality of the foul contefted by fome, and openly denied by others? And were not the duties of morality imperfectly underftood, and the boundaries of right and wrong inaccurately defined?

But it is not my intention to enlarge upon thefe topics at prefent; I referve them for fuller difcuffion hereafter, and I am content to reft the neceffity of the Chriftian Revelation fimply upon the want of certain knowledge with refpect to a future life.

It will fcarcely be denied, except it be by thofe who in the pride of human reafon difdain the control of an omnifcient God, the Creator, Governor, and Judge of mankind, and give us in his ftead a Being of their own creation—except it be by fuch, it will fcarcely at this time be denied, that the certainty of a future life, and a future ftate of retribution, is the vital principle of all religion and all virtue. Take away the

hope

hope of a future exiftence, and we lofe all proper motives for piety to God, or benevolence to man. What can fupport us amidft the unequal difpenfations of this life, or give us fortitude to endure its difappointments, its difficulties, and its forrows, but the affurance of future recompence? And what can induce us to refift the impulfe of paffion, and the importunate cravings of appetite, if, when this tranfitory fcene is clofed, we are to go, without the fear of punifhment, or the hope of reward, to the everlafting home of the ancient Epicurean, or the eternal fleep of the modern Atheift?

If then the knowledge, not only of a future ftate of exiftence, but a future ftate of rewards and punifhments, be indifpenfably neceffary to our happinefs, do we know of any fyftem of religion, that exprefsly promifed fuch a ftate to us, before the Gofpel had brought life and immortality to light? If the promife had been given any where, we fhould naturally expect to find it in Judaifm, a religion unqueftionably from heaven: but there it is

not

not—the promise of eternal life is not amongst the rewards of the Mosaic Law[g]: the favoured agent of God is empowered to enforce his decrees by the promise of temporal prosperity in case of obedience, and the denunciation of dreadful visitations, of plagues, famine, and desolation, in case of disobedience: but of future rewards, or future punishments, no mention is made.

Doubtless under the Law, as under every other dispensation, holy and virtuous men, either by their own reflections, or by the especial grace of God imparted to them, were led to expect another state, which would account for the evils and the disorders of the present. The holy Scriptures abound with passages, which will scarcely admit of any other interpretation [h]: and it is certainly reasonable to suppose, that the opinions of good and pious men upon such a subject would influence in a great degree the popular belief: but we are not to

---

[g] Bp. Bull's Harmonia Apostolica, Diss. Post. Chap. X.
[h] See the passages cited by Jortin in his Dissertation on a Future State.

SERMON I.

conclude from thence, that the notion of a future state was either generally admitted, or accurately underſtood.

Of the two great ſects who led the Synagogues, one openly denied the poſſibility of a reſurrection; and the other, although it allowed that a departed ſoul might reanimate another body, was far from imagining that the ſame perſon would riſe again from the grave, to account for the works done in the body, and to receive reward or puniſhment.

What the Almighty did not think fit clearly and explicitly to reveal to his choſen people, it would be in vain to aſk of thoſe who were left to the guidance of their own unaſſiſted reaſon. Political ſecurity was the great object of Gentile religion, ſo that whilſt expiatory ſacrifices, luſtrations, and coſtly offerings were allowed to be a ſufficient atonement for the vices of the opulent, the idea of futurity was blended with fable and allegory, to amuſe the idle, and with abſurd terrors and fanciful puniſhments, to terrify the vulgar. The ſtateſman

man derided in secret what he publicly sanctioned; and even they who could not but indulge the pleasing hope of immortality, even the best and wisest amongst them, seem rather to have cherished the idea with a fond and anxious wish that it might be realized, than with any thing like conviction or certainty that it would be so.

Since then neither the light of reason, nor the light of revelation, afforded any certainty upon this important point, nothing at best but a hope and a persuasion; since the natural law written in the heart of man was only to be discovered by the labour of the virtuous few, and even they acknowledged its inefficacy; whilst the generality of mankind were given up to the gross errors of popular superstition and idolatrous worship, living in the world without the knowledge of God, or the expectation of futurity; it cannot surely at this time be doubted whether a more explicit revelation was necessary. Ought we not rather to offer up continual thanks to God, for having poured down upon us the

SERMON I.

the glorious light of his Gofpel, for having in his good time revealed even unto babes what was fo long " hidden from the wife and prudent[1];" for having given us, not the hope or expectation merely, but the affurance of happinefs, and having made us, not the believers only, but the heirs of immortality.

But if it be granted that no prior knowledge fuperfeded the ufe of a more explicit revelation, and that upon this ground Chriftianity was neceffary, then the other parts of the objection are preffed upon us with greater force—Why was the communication of truths fo effential to our happinefs fo long delayed? Where was the neceffity for a preparatory difpenfation? And why is not the light of the Gofpel at this day impartially diffufed over the whole race of mankind.

In reply to queftions of this fort, it would perhaps be fufficient fimply to plead our

[1] Matt. xi. 25. Luke x. 21.

ignorance of the counsels of God: " it is not for us to know the times, or the seasons, which the Father hath put into his own power[k]." Our ignorance of the motives and the causes, which God hath chosen to conceal from our view, is so very obvious, every occurrence of common life, and every phenomenon of nature, so unquestionably prove it, that the proudest reasoner need not be ashamed to confess his weakness: the meek and lowly mind avows it with gladness, because in its own feebleness and the power of God it sees the true and proper grounds of faith, of confidence in the promises of God, and of rational acquiescence in the wisdom of his dispensations.

Christianity is called by the Apostles, the " dispensation of the fulness of time[l]," " the mystery reserved for the latter days:" and the terms " latter days[m]," and " latter ages," which so frequently occur in the

[k] Acts i. 7. [l] Ephes. i. 10.
[m] Joel ii. 28. Acts ii. 17. Heb. i. 2. 1 Pet. i. 5. 20.

writers

SERMON I. 15

writers both of the Old and New Testament, the Jewish Church always understood to refer to the days of their promised Messiah. The Holy Spirit seems to have characterized that period of time by such an appellation, because the Gospel of Christ was to contain the last instruction of God to man, " to close the book, to seal up the vision and the prophecy, and to bring in everlasting righteousness[n]."

In this sense the expression is plain and appropriate; but no man can with justice apply the relative term lateness to the first preaching of the Gospel, unless it be in his power to ascertain the proportion which the age of Tiberius bears to the future, as well as to the past, and to determine for how many ages the Creator intends that the fabric of the universe and all that is in it should subsist; and since this cannot be done, since the " terrible day of the Lord," for wise and merciful reasons, is shrouded in darkness; for this reason only it is absurd to pronounce of

[n] Dan. ix. 24.

any revelation, that it cannot be from God, becaufe, according to our notions of time, it was revealed too late.

Surely if God be omnipotent and infinite, and man finite and dependent, it is as unreafonable for man to fay, that God fhall deliver his commands at this or that particular time, and to refufe obedience to them becaufe they come either fooner or later than he thinks right, as it would be to prefcribe what the fubject of the commands fhould be, and what the mode in which they fhould be delivered. In the wonderful and unfearchable plans of Omnifcience, there muft, from their very nature, be many hidden motives, which will elude the utmoft keennefs of human penetration, and many reafons for delay, which are known to him alone, with whom " a thoufand years are as one day, and one day as a thoufand years°;" for thefe reafons it would be vain to fearch. But even from our own partial and limited view of God's defigns, from our own obfervation of

° 2 Pet. iii. 8.

the

the conftant analogies of his government, and the ufual courfe of his Providence, we may infer, that fuch a difpenfation, as we know Chriftianity to be, could not have been revealed to any effectual purpofe at an earlier period of fociety.

Through the whole order of creation, and the whole fcheme of Providence, we obferve marks of a progreffive advancement and a gradual difcovery of truth. In all the operations of the human mind, in the important difcoveries of art, and the improvements of laws and government, we go on ftep by ftep, as leifure and opportunities offer, or new wants are created, until at laft we have completely filled up the firft rude outline which neceffity fuggefted. A fimilar progrefs is to be obferved in the higher and more valuable truths of religion; and God Almighty, in mercy and love to his creatures, feems always to have proportioned his difcoveries, not only to the actual wants of mankind, but to their capacity of receiving truth themfelves, and their means of communicating it to others.

In the infancy of the world, God conversed personally with man; and as often as the uncertainty inseparable from traditional communications, or the perverseness and corruption of human nature, had destroyed the force of his commands, and obliterated the memory of his promises, he interposed continually to rescue " a righteous seed" from the general depravity; he confirmed their wavering faith by a renewal of his covenants, and satisfied their doubts by a display of supernatural power. But, as their numbers increased, neither the warnings of his Almighty voice, nor the continual manifestations of his power; nor even his sensible presence in glory amongst them, were sufficient to retain his chosen people in a firm reliance upon his word, and a steady obedience to his precepts. Suppose that the Gospel had been preached, without any preparatory discipline, to men thus rooted as it were to the earth, unused to any thing like abstract reasoning, and unable to raise their minds from the objects of sense which surrounded them; is it at all credible that they would have embraced a system of religion, whose

SERMON I.   19

whose essential character is its spirituality? which teaches us, that " the Lord of heaven and earth, the Lofty One that inhabiteth eternity[p]," is a Spirit; that he desires " to be worshipped in spirit and in truth[q];" and that the silent devotion of the heart is more grateful to him than all the magnificence of ceremonious worship, the costly shrine, the pompous offering, and the blood of ten thousand victims.

Again, Christianity was to be universal; it was not to be a local worship, or a partial institution, but was designed to extend its blessed influence over the whole race of mankind. How then was it to be generally propagated, before any mode had been devised of conveying instruction to distant countries, or remote posterity? Tradition, the only source of information which the early ages possessed, was sufficient for them; few in number, and closely connected by affinity, by alliance, and by situation; at a time too when the period of human life was extended so far beyond its present

[p] Isai. lvii. 15.   [q] John iv. 23.

limits,

limits, it was eafy for a family or a tribe, to tranfmit to their pofterity any truth, or any fact, without miftake or material alteration.

But when population increafed, when colonies were fettled in diftant regions, and unconnected ftates were rifing into power, tradition loft its ufe, and the inftructions which it had conveyed were gradually forgotten. No important leffons could then be given for general ufe, until new channels of communication were opened, until the earth was not only peopled but civilized, until found philofophy had prepared the mind for the ftudy of abftract truths, and the familiar ufe of letters had fupplied the means of making them public.

Thus, from the character of Chriftianity itfelf, and from the general influence which it was intended to have over the world, it may fairly be argued, that the mercy of God was as confpicuous in delaying the bleffing fo long, as it was in giving it at all; and, from what our own experience teaches

teaches us, from the infight which we are permitted to have into the divine counfels, partial and imperfect as it is, it may alfo be argued, that, had not the blefling been delayed fo long, it would have failed of its intended effect; unlefs indeed we fuppofe a conftant miracle to have attended its progrefs, and an overruling control to have fupported it; which, had it been the cafe, would have fuperfeded the ufe of human reafon, have deftroyed the free agency, and confequently the refponfibility of man, and have taken away all the merit of a rational faith, a faith founded upon conviction.

From the period of its promulgation therefore, which hereafter I fhall fhew to have been the moft proper that could have been devifed, and, from the gradual preparation for its eftablifhment, we might infer the divine origin of Chriftianity on this ground merely, that the time and the preparation, if properly confidered, reconcile the foreknowledge of God with the freedom of man. And here I would be content to leave the fubject for the prefent, were it not neceſſary to notice another queſtion, of high importance, which is frequently obtruded upon us. Suppoſing that a knowledge of the Chriſtian doctrines be neceſſary to eternal happineſs, what is to become of thoſe who lived before they were revealed? or of thoſe to whom the glad tidings of peace and ſalvation as yet have not been preached?

Here, as before, we might fairly plead our ignorance of the counſels of God, our reluctance to pry with eager curioſity into that which is hidden from us, and our diſpoſition to be contented with that which is plainly revealed. Simple and honeſt minds, which are ſolicitous only for truth, will gladly admit the validity of ſuch a plea: but ſimplicity and ſingleneſs of mind are not the virtues of the enemies of our faith.

In the declamations of the Heathen ſophiſts, from whom our own Deiſtical writers have liberally borrowed, we find frequent compariſons between the intolerance of Chriſtianity and the liberal ſpirit of Paganiſm.

ganism. Christians declared, that they would have no share in the celebration of Heathen mysteries; they avowed their abhorrence of their sacrifices, and steadily refused to bow down before their idols; therefore they were persecuted as the enemies of mankind, as devoting to endless perdition all but the friends of their own sect, and the converts to their own worship.

But was this ever a just accusation? Far from it; Christians, it is true, from the very first publication of the Gospel, have uniformly declared, that to inherit eternal salvation, we must have faith in Jesus Christ—that he is the "only Mediator between God and man'"—that "eternal life is the gift of God, through him^s"—and "that there is no other name given under heaven, by which man can be saved^t."

But do Christians condemn, or, if fu-

^r 1 Tim. ii. 5. ^s Rom. vi. 23.
^t Acts iv. 12.

rious and bigoted zealots have ever done so, is it in Christianity to condemn those, to whom these truths were never known? It cannot be—we pray indeed, that it would please the Almighty to soften the hearts, and to enlighten the understandings, of all his creatures: but God forbid, that we should presume to set bounds to his compassion, or to say how far his mercy and patient abiding shall be continued.

For those indeed, who, having once received the word, voluntarily apostatize from it; who vilify and traduce the Revelation itself, as if it were the invention of man, and not the word of God; and who labour, by false representations of its history, and perverse interpretations of its doctrines, to lessen its *practical* influence upon mankind; for those, we do pronounce, upon the authority of our holy Teacher and his Apostles, that the bitterness of wrath is reserved, and that, when he shall hereafter appear in glory, the Lord will cast them out from his presence, to the punishment they have deserved.

But

But we never assert, that ignorance will be a reason for condemnation; we have been taught, what is strictly conformable to our notions of the goodness and mercy of God, by those, " to whom it was given to see the mysteries of heaven"—we have been taught, that every allowance will be made for involuntary ignorance; that a " man is accepted according to that he hath, not according to that he hath not[x]," and that, in God's good time, the Religion of Christ will become universal: and, till that glorious event takes place, we conclude that the merits of his death extend their influence even to those who still remain in the darkness and shadow of death.

With what confidence, then, can it be asserted, that God is either partial in his discoveries of truth, or unjust in his promises of happiness? Or upon what principle can it be maintained, that a revelation cannot be divine, because it was gradually opened, and is not yet universal? when our reason teaches us, that such a

---

[x] 2 Cor. iii. 12.

revelation could not have been communicated in any other way, confiftently with the general tenor of God's government; and the revelation itfelf exprefsly declares, that neither its promifes nor its threatenings are limited, that futurity will prove its impartiality, and that, when the veil is withdrawn from our eyes, all apparent inequalities will be done away.

The very delay then, which is complained of, is, as I have remarked before, the ftrongeft argument, both of the wifdom of God, and the juftice of God; of his wifdom, in proceeding flowly and filently, by the operation of fecond caufes, to the fulfilment of his eternal purpofe; of his juftice, in accumulating, for the conviction of man, fuch an unbroken feries of teftimony, that no fophiftry will ever be able to prevail againft it.

Confiftency of conduct, and uniformity of defign, we always confider as infallible criteria of wifdom. We admire the fagacity of mind, which can promptly choofe a wife end; the difcernment, which can

felect

select the properest means for executing it; and the fortitude, which can go on steadily to its completion, in defiance of difficulty or opposition. And in all the concerns of human life, our opinion of man's wisdom rises in proportion to the excellency of the end proposed, and the difficulty of the means which lead to success.

Doubtless it will be granted, that the human imagination can conceive no end equal in magnitude and importance to the *redemption of mankind*: and if it be possible from the earliest times, and the very first act of guilt and disobedience to God, to trace a plan, uniformly tending to the accomplishment of this great design; if it can be proved, from the eventful history of one nation, that the frame of their government, their peculiar institutions, and the ritual of their worship, were all in fact preparatory to this design: whilst the strange reverses of their fortunes, and their frequent vicissitudes, from power and opulence, to captivity and desolation, all contributed to promote it—if, meanwhile, the same governing principle be found to control

trol the fates of other people, and the revolutions of other empires; if Affyria, Perfia, Macedon, and Rome, in purfuing their own ambitious fchemes of conqueft and dominion, are only the blind agents in the general fcheme of Providence, "howbeit they meant not fo, neither did their heart think fo [y];" if all this can be proved, from the undoubted evidence of hiftory, we may boldly afk the Infidel, whether it does not become him to cry out, with the Egyptian Magi of old, "this is the finger of God[z]."

[y] Ifai. x. 7.   [z] Exod. viii. 19.

SERMON II.

EZEKIEL xxxvi. 22.

I DO NOT THIS FOR YOUR SAKES, O HOUSE OF ISRAEL, BUT FOR MINE HOLY NAME'S SAKE.

THE holy Prophet was permitted to forefee, not only the conqueft and captivity of his brethren, but their fubfequent deliverance and reftoration to their native country. They were to fuffer, he tells them, for their iniquities, for their neglect of the worfhip which God himfelf had prefcribed to them, and their attachment to the idolatries of Moab and Ammon. But the juftice of God would in time be fatisfied; they were to return to Judæa, with a new heart and a new fpirit;

rit; God was to be again their God, and they were to be again his people; and this was to take place, this signal inſtance of Divine mercy was to be exhibited to the world, not for their ſakes, He reminds them, but for the ſake of God's holy name.

To glorify his name, to teach mankind, that is, not only that there is a Creator and Governor of the univerſe, infinite in power and knowledge; but that there is and can be only one ſuch Being, and that He alone is the proper object of human worſhip; and to eſtabliſh the important doctrine on the indiſputable authority of Revelation, as it was the chief ground and motive for all the viciſſitudes in the fortunes of the Jewiſh people, ſo it was the firſt ſtep in the ſcheme of God's providence, when He ſummoned the faithful Abraham from an idolatrous country and an idolatrous family, when He confirmed his belief by the evidence of works, which human power never could have effected, and rewarded his obedience by the promiſe, mife, that "in his feed all the nations of the earth fhould be bleffed[a]."

An attempt to demonftrate the unity of the eternal Godhead would be foreign to my defign: but it is of importance to confider, how it happened, that a truth, revealed to the primitive ages, and difcoverable in all ages by the deductions of human reafon, was gradually corrupted, and loft, as to all practical purpofes, amidft the wild dreams and monftrous inventions of Polytheifm; and why it was neceffary, as a preparatory ftep, to the introduction of Chriftianity, that the knowledge of the only true God, the folid rock upon which the fabric of all true religion muft be raifed, fhould be taught and maintained, not in an obfcure corner, or a fmall and infignificant community, but in the eftablifhed worfhip of a numerous people, connected, as has been well obferved, either as allies, as tributaries, or as fubjects, with every part of the civilized world.

[a] Gen. xxii. 18.

SERMON II.

In reviewing the history of Religion, it is a point of extreme nicety and difficulty, to distinguish exactly between the discoveries of reason and the remains of early tradition. Man is undoubtedly, in the very frame and constitution of his nature, a religious being; God has given him a consciousness of dependence and inferiority, a natural anxiety to discover the will of his superior, and a natural inclination to offer up his adoration and thanksgiving, for the blessings which he enjoys. Feeling this natural impulse within us, and having long been taught to direct it in a reasonable service to its proper object, we are apt perhaps to think better of our own powers than we ought, and to call some truths, truths of natural Religion, which are in reality the Revelations of God. It is, at all events, wiser and safer to attribute more to God, than to man; and if we consider as a matter of fact, what our own reason has done, we shall indeed be little inclined to prize it too highly.

" God," as the Apostle tells us, certainly
" never

SERMON II.

" never left himfelf without a witnefs[b]." From the mighty works of his creation, it was at all times eafy to infer his power; from their beauty and utility, his goodnefs; and from their order, fymmetry, and regularity, his unity.

So far it was the voice of nature, and the concurrent opinion of all mankind, that there is one fupreme God, the Maker, Preferver, and Governor of the world; and this may with ftrict propriety be called the Religion of Nature.

But when it came to be a queftion, how the Supreme Being conducted his government, then began the grand miftake, from which all the abfurdities of Paganifm date their origin: for, while the Deity was fuppofed to be fhrouded in his own ineffable majefty, and abforbed in the contemplation of his own glory, he was beheld at an awful diftance, as the object of fear and apprehenfion, rather than of love. The contemplation of his Power, and his Pro-

[b] Acts xiv. 17.

vidence, in fuftaining and regulating the complicated fyftem of nature, did not lead, as it might have done, by fair and rational analogy, to juft notions of his moral government; the clofe and intimate relation which fubfifts between God and man, as the Creator and the creature, was entirely overlooked; and all accefs to the one Supreme was denied to man, except through the interceffion of his delegates, the fubordinate deities, who were fuppofed to be the interpreters of his will, and the minifters of his power.

From this fource were derived all the fictions of Polytheifm, and all the grofs and abominable corruptions of fymbolical worfhip. It was not that the exiftence of God was denied, or his Providence controverted, but that his unity was changed into a preeminence in rank and authority over a multitude of imaginary beings, who were reprefented as the agents and mediators between God and man; his holy and incommunicable name was profaned by an union with idols; his worfhip was affociated with theirs, and the glory due only to to him was lavishly bestowed upon the very lowest of his creatures.

The sacred Historian has not precisely marked the first rise of idolatrous worship; but he has told us that it began early, and that, in defiance of repeated admonitions, the idolaters continued to increase in number, and in wickedness, till " the measure of their iniquity was full;" they were then swept away from the face of the earth, by that great and awful dispensation, which has stamped upon the form and the substance of the material world, indelible marks of the power of the Creator.

It was not long however before the descendants of the " righteous remnant," who had been saved, forgot the miraculous preservation of their ancestors; and as soon as they had separated from each other, and had settled in the countries allotted to them by the especial appointment of God, we find them almost immediately relapsing into the very iniquities which had brought upon their forefathers so terrible a punishment.

When the memory of early revelations was lost, and the Almighty had withdrawn himself from immediate communication with his creatures, nature taught them to look up to the heavenly bodies, whose splendor was the continual object of their admiration, and whose utility their daily experience testified. In these glorious luminaries they fixed the residence of those ideal beings, to whom they had assigned the office of mediation and intercession with the Supreme Lord of the creation.

Planetary worship then was the first step in the career of falsehood; and it was accompanied, as in rude and uncivilized societies it naturally would be, not with the cheerful piety, and rational awe, which true Religion inspires, but with the restless and harassing apprehensions of superstition; with sudden and unexpected changes from hope to disappointment, and from joy and gladness to dismay and despair.

Against

Against this dreadful state of doubt and apprehension, the Holy Spirit warns the chosen people of Israel: " Learn not the ways of the Heathen," says the Prophet, " and be not dismayed at the signs of heaven, for the Heathen are dismayed at them [c]."

The effects of this superstition upon the mind were as various as the vicissitudes of the elements are various and inconstant; at one time the face of nature is serene and tranquil; at another, the sky is black with darkness; the heavenly bodies withdraw their influence, and the storm and the hurricane spread desolation around.

Hence arose the distinction of good and evil demons, of whom the former were supposed to dispense to man the blessings of the Creator, health, and plenty, and fruitful seasons; the latter, his punishments, sickness, and plague, and famine. Hence too it happened, that if men were at one time disposed to adore the Creator,

[c] Jer. ix. 14.

as the beneficent Father of the univerſe, the Parent of good, impartially ſhowering down his gifts upon all; at another, they turned from him with dread and apprehenſion, as a moroſe, tyrannical Being, ſporting with the miſeries of mortals, who delighted in gloomy and myſterious rites, and whoſe fury was to be appeaſed by the blood of his creatures.

To the worſhip of the heavenly bodies ſuccceded that of deified men, following, it ſhould ſeem, in a natural order, the progreſs of civilization, and the improvements of ſocial life; for deified men were the founders of colonies, the inventors of uſeful arts, the legiſlators, who by wiſdom had curbed the impetuoſity of man, and taught him the great duty of ſubmiſſion to legal authority, and the heroes, who by their valour had extended the dominion and increaſed the proſperity of their native country.

Gratitude for benefits received might perhaps be the original motive for worſhipping the benefactor; but pride and vanity

nity perpetuated what gratitude began; and while the people offered their incenfe at the fhrines of the heroes, whofe actions they had been taught to venerate, the defcendants of the illuftrious characters gloried in the poffeffion of ftatues, and genealogies, which authenticated their alliance to Divinity.

From the union of thefe two branches of idolatrous worfhip arofe a third, a ftrange and motley compound, which defcended to the adoration of attributes, and paffions, of vices and virtues, and even of plants and animals[d].

Such is the general outline of the rife and progrefs of Gentile idolatry; the origin is ever the fame; and however it might fometimes affume more brilliancy of ornament to pleafe the eye, and more feducing allurements to fafcinate the imagination, and to corrupt the paffions, the fame

---

[d] For a fuller view of the origin and progrefs of idolatrous worfhip, the reader is referred to the " Divine Legation of Mofes Demonftrated." Book iv. fect. 4.

general principle may be traced from the Sabian idolatry of Chaldea, through the polluted channel of Egyptian superstition, until we see it under all the advantages of beautiful poetry, and the pageantry of games and festivals, in the temples of Greece and Rome.

To give more than the general outline is not necessary to my argument; and were it necessary, I should be loth, before an audience of Scholars, to enter into a detail which the general course of their studies has familiarized to them; and, God knows, it is at all times a painful task to pursue the wanderings of the human mind through such an inextricable labyrinth of error and absurdity.

But where, it may be asked, amidst such a multiplicity of imaginary Deities, whilst "ᵉ the glory of the incorruptible God was changed into an image made like to corruptible man, and to birds, and four footed beasts, and creeping things"—where

ᵉ Rom. i. 23.

was

was the notion to be found of one Supreme God, which even the Heathen world had not entirely loft, although "ᶠknowing God, they worfhipped him not as God?"

The belief, or the perfuafion then, for I by no means affert that it was a juft and accurate knowledge, exifted in the colleges of the priefts, and the fchools of the philofophers; and of the philofophers, the weakeft declared, that variety of worfhip muft be grateful to a Being delighting in the concord and harmony of his works. The wifeft maintained, that a myfterious veil muft be thrown over the awful truth, which was too excellent for vulgar minds to comprehend: and the priefts meanwhile carefully fecluded from general notice a doctrine, which, had it been publicly avowed, would have expofed the fallacy of their auguries, their oracles, their vows, and their facrifices, and have demolifhed at one blow the whole fabric of gainful fuperftition.

ᶠ Rom. i. 21.

Thus,

Thus, while in the one cafe upon principle, and in the other from felf-intereft, the knowledge of God was hidden in the dark and impenetrable fhade of myfteries, the uninitiated multitude were left to the uncontrouled indulgence of their paffions. At all times, and under all circumftances, fymbolical worfhip has been accompanied by corrupt and profligate morals; it is eafy to fee why it muft be fo; it follows neceffarily and immediately, as a confequence of that miftake which I have ftated to be the original caufe of Polytheifm—the notion of fubordinate Deities, who have their feparate and diftinct offices affigned to them under the one Supreme Caufe, in the adminiftration and government of the world.

Moral virtue confifts in the practice of thofe duties which our relative fituation in fociety demand; and thofe duties are of indifpenfable obligation, becaufe it is the will of God that his creatures fhould fo act, as to promote the happinefs of each other. But a variety of Gods may, and perhaps neceffarily muft, produce a variety

of

of wills; and then it becomes a queftion, who is to be obeyed? And if we go a ftep farther, and fuppofe it poffible that the example of any of thofe Gods fhould be vicious, then we muft conclude it to be their will, that man fhould be vicious alfo: and in this way we may account for that black and dreadful catalogue of vices, which the Apoftles continually enumerate in their pictures of the Gentile world.

Such then being the ftate of by far the greater part of the world, when our Saviour entered upon his public miniftry, if the reprefentation which I have given of their worfhip and their practice be juft, what can we fuppofe would have been the fate of our holy Religion, unlefs the wifdom of Providence in the general depravity had preferved a chofen feed, who, " although their hearts were hardened, and their underftandings darkened," blindly accomplifhed the purpofes of his will, by preferving in the volumes of their Religion, the hiftory of the early Revelations, on which the Gofpel was founded, and by

adoring

adoring in their public worship none but the God of their fathers, the Holy One of Israel?

To establish a new religion in any case must be a work of great difficulty; but to establish it upon the ruins of inveterate prejudices, and of opinions sanctioned by time, and by habit; to tell men, that all that they have hitherto been taught is false, and that all the impressions which their education has given them are nothing more than " lying vanities;" instead of granting them the free indulgence of their inclinations and their appetites, to impose rigid and severe restraints upon both; to expose the nothingness of the fairest ideal picture of virtue, and the brightest exterior semblance of morality; and to require truth and purity in the inward parts; all this is a task surpassing the powers of a human teacher, and this was the task of Christ and his Apostles.

Let us suppose then that a person had come with this design, not to Jerusalem, but to any of the celebrated cities of the Gen-

Gentiles, to Corinth, Athens, or Rome; that, without any previous expectation of his appearance, he had announced himself as the meffenger of God; let his addrefs be made, not to the wealthy, the powerful, or the wife, but, as our bleffed Saviour's actually was, to the poor, the lowly, and the ignorant; let him command them, with the tone and authority of a teacher fent from God, to give up their eftablifhed belief, to quit their former habits, to repent of their fins, and to be converted;—what would have been the effect, is it probable, of fuch a fummons? If they had been able to reftrain their indignation, at hearing that the Deities, which they had long been accuftomed to reverence and adore, were now to be forfaken and defpifed; if there had been calmnefs and moderation enough to reafon and argue upon the fubject, would not the firft queftion have been, Who is the God you fpeak of, and what is his name?

Here then it would have been neceffary, in the firft inftance, to have proved

the

the exiftence of one Supreme God, the Creator and Governor of the univerfe; to have proved his attributes, his power, his wifdom, and his juftice; to have proved, in fhort, all the great truths of natural Religion, upon which Chriftianity is founded.

You tell us, they would have faid, that you are a meffenger from God; convince us therefore, firft, that the God you call upon us to obey really exifts; that he did, as you pretend, create the univerfe by his power; and that he now fuftains, directs, and governs it by his Providence; and then it will be time for us to confider, whether the fyftem which you offer us be really his revealed will, or not.

But let us change the fcene, and obferve our bleffed Lord addreffing himfelf to the inhabitants of Jerufalem: here he came to his own. The foundation of the religion which he defigned to teach was already laid in the popular opinions, and the national faith. The unity of God was acknowledged by all ranks and all defcriptions

SERMON II. 47

scriptions of men; a call to repentance excited no astonishment, and caused no prejudice, in the first instance, against his doctrines, because it was immediately connected with all the legal ceremonies of their Religion, and all the principal facts of their history; and a claim to the office and character of a Messiah in the first instance prepossessed them in favour of the person who made it, because all the Prophets had given them the promise of a deliverer; and it was the first and fondest wish of their hearts, to witness the accomplishment.

"Let the counsel of the Holy One of Israel draw nigh[g], and where is the promise of his coming[h]?" were become almost proverbial expressions amongst the Jews; so that a teacher, calling himself the Christ, was certain at least of finding hearers ready to attend to his instructions, and eager to examine his pretensions. Then there was time to observe his character and his conduct; to discuss the nature of his miracles,

[g] Isaiah v. 19.   [h] 2 Pet. ii. 3, 4.

and

and to feel the intrinsic purity of his doctrines, and the superior force of his arguments, till at length a body of witnesses was formed; then it was immaterial, as to its progress, that is, and its future success, whether the nation at large admitted the new Religion, or not; indeed their very rejection of it was, as it turned out, a convincing argument of its truth.

It was with a view therefore to guard the fundamental doctrines of Revelation from the contagion of falsehood, and, by so doing, to aid and assist the first publication of the Gospel, that God thought fit to separate the Jewish nation from the rest of mankind; that he favoured them, above all other people, by disclosing to them, from time to time, "the deep and secret things of his wisdom;" and that he made them the depositaries of truth, by committing to their custody the living oracles of his word.

In what manner this separation was effected, and by what admirable methods the Providence of God contrived to interweave

SERMON II.

weave and connect their establishment as a church, with their civil polity as a state, and to make the religious code of the former both the history and the legal institutes of the latter, so that no suspicion of fraud or forgery can, with any reason, be urged against either, is a point of such material importance, that it deserves a separate discussion: I shall reserve it therefore for a future discourse.

It cannot, meanwhile, be expected, that I should enter into a formal refutation of the frivolous cavils, and, to call them by no worse a name, the poor and vulgar jests, with which free-thinking philosophers have attacked the scheme of a favoured people, as if God could have any favourites, but those who love and obey him, and whose principal aim it is, "to do justly, to love mercy, and to walk humbly before him[i];" or as if the Father of mankind, whose mercy is over all his works, could have shut up the knowledge of himself within the narrow precincts of a particular church, unless it had been with a

[i] Micah vi. 8.

design,

design, worthy indeed of his care, and becoming the wisdom of his Providence, upon the same foundation gradually to erect the universal Church of Christ.

The sentence of the Prophet, which I have quoted in my text, explains the whole œconomy: " It is not for your sakes, O house of Israel, that I do this, but for mine holy Name's sake[k]." It is not on account of your own merits, or for the sake of your own prosperity, that I have distinguished you with peculiar marks of my favour; but it is to glorify my great name, that all the world may see and confess, that I am indeed the true God, and that there is none other beside me.

[k] Ezek. xxxvi. 22.

SERMON III.

NUMBERS xxiii. 9.

LO, THE PEOPLE SHALL DWELL ALONE, AND SHALL NOT BE RECKONED AMONGST THE NATIONS.

HAVING shewn in my former Discourse, that, if Polytheism had been universal, Christianity could not have been promulged, and that it pleased the Almighty, for that reason, to separate the Jewish nation from the rest of mankind, in order to make them the guardians of his Revelations, I now proceed to lay before you a view of the methods by which that separation was effected.

SERMON III.

[a] The Prophet of Midian was fummoned by the King of Moab, in the true fpirit of idolatry, to imprecate the vengeance of heaven upon the chofen people; but the Holy Spirit gave him utterance, and he bleffed where he was defired to curfe. He forefaw, through the whole courfe of their eventful hiftory, the marked difcrimination of their character, the peculiarity of their government, and their refidence in the promifed land under the immediate protection of God; and in terms of benediction fimilar to thofe which were ufed by their own Patriarch [b], and their own Legiflator [c], he pronounced that "Ifrael fhould dwell alone." As there was at that time no probability, humanly fpeaking, that the Ifraelites would ever be able to expel the inhabitants of the country which they were going to invade, and even if we fuppofe that conqueft to have been probable, as a diftinct and feparate exiftence is contrary to all the maxims of human policy, and to the natural inclinations and wifhes of the

---

[a] Numb. xxii.
[b] Gen. xlix. 8.
[c] Deut. xxxiii. 28.

human

human heart, which lead nations, as well as individuals, to intercourse and commerce, and affociation with each other, nothing but the forefight of God could have conceived the poffibility of fo extraordinary a fact, and nothing lefs than the power and the wifdom of God could have brought it to pafs.

Let us fee then how the Almighty contrived, whilft all other nations were tending to union and connexion with each other, and prided themfelves upon the community of their religion, to keep his peculiar people at a diftance from all others, and to make even their vices and their prejudices fubfervient to the purpofes of feparation and diftinction.

The government of the Jews differed from every other government in this fundamental point; that the fupreme power of the ftate refided neither in a man, nor in a body of men, but in God: whatever title, or whatever authority, was given to their chief magiftrates, whether they were Judges, Kings, or High Priefts, they were ftrictly and properly

perly the delegates of the Supreme God. Thus there was no distinction whatever between their establishment as a church, and their constitution as a political body; for the laws, which were framed to secure and preserve the worship of the one true God, were in fact the civil laws of the people, and a branch of their political government.

Such were the terms of the original covenant between God and his people. He had chosen them for his subjects, as well as his worshippers; and they had acknowledged him for their King, as well as their God. " Say to them," was the command of the Almighty to Moses, " say to them, If ye will obey my voice, and keep my covenant, then ye shall be a peculiar treasure to me above all people; ye shall be unto me a kingdom of priests, and an holy nation [d]:" and the answer of the people was, " All that the Lord hath spoken, that will we do [e]."

In all human societies, obedience to the

[d] Exod. xix. 5.   [e] Exod. xix. 8.

SERMON III.

laws which protect him is the virtue of the citizen; in the Theocracy of the Jews, it was his religion: for, as their own Historian tells us, Moses did not make Religion a part of virtue; but moral virtue, justice, that is, temperance, and fortitude, good order, and all the great duties which cement and consolidate the fabric of civil society, the Divine Legislator made parts of Religion[f].

Here then at once there is a manifest distinction between the people of God and all other nations, in the very essential and fundamental articles of their constitution: a distinction, necessarily caused by the primary design and end of their separation; which, as we have seen, was to preserve the pure worship of the one invisible God, and to transmit to posterity all the great truths of Religion, which naturally flow from that source.

God then being the Supreme Magistrate of their state, idolatry, which was an express violation of the compact between

---

[f] Josephus contra Apion, lib. ii. sect. 16.

the Governor and the governed, a transgreſſion, as it is called, of the covenant, was puniſhed with the ſame rigour with which human legiſlators have at all times, and in all ages, juſtly puniſhed acts of treaſon and rebellion againſt the ſovereign authority of the ſtate.

Wherever the Iſraelite came, he was to aſſert the great and glorious name of Jehovah, to proclaim the iniquity of worſhipping ſtrange Gods, to break down their images, to deſtroy their groves, and trample upon their altars; and with the idolaters themſelves, if they perſiſted in their crimes, he was to form no league or treaty whatever, to ſhew them no mercy or compaſſion, but to ſmite and utterly deſtroy them.

And if amongſt his own people, or his own tribe, or even in the boſom of his own family, any inclination ſhould be found to emulate the corruptions of his neighbours, or any attempt be made to ſeduce him from his allegiance to the only true God, he is commanded to puniſh inſtantly;

stantly; neither the habits of long and familiar acquaintance, nor the endearments of friendship, nor even the ties of filial and parental affection, are to withhold his hand from striking the blow. " If thy brother, the son of thy mother, or thy son, or thy daughter entice thee secretly, saying, Let us go and serve other Gods, which thou hast not known, thou shalt not consent unto him, nor hearken unto him; neither shall thine eye pity him; but thou shalt surely kill him, because he hath thought to thrust thee away from the Lord thy God [g]."

Thus the great distinction of Religion was enforced by the positive prohibition of all community of worship with idolaters, even by the express command of extirpating them wherever they existed; and upon their steady and faithful perseverance in the worship of the God of their fathers, depended entirely their possession of the country which he had given to them, the peace and happiness of individuals, and the general prosperity of their empire.

[g] Deut. xiii. 6—9.

To forbid, under severe penalties, what others love and cultivate, is the severest method of drawing a boundary between those we wish to separate: thus the Jews were expressly commanded not to pass their children through the fire, like the barbarous worshippers of Moloch [h]; not to disfigure or wound their bodies, like the followers of Baal; not to perform the acts of devotion in high places, in gloomy caverns, or obscure recesses; nor throw the shade of mystery over their worship, by planting impenetrable groves in the neighbourhood of their tabernacles [i].

But whilst all imitation of the horrid rites of their neighbours, and the absurd superstition of other nations, was expressly prohibited to the Jews, God gave them a ritual and a practical system of worship, which of itself was eminently calculated to gain upon their minds, and to secure them from the contagion of Polytheism.

In the days of the Patriarchs the pompous and majestic display of ceremonious

---

[h] Levit. xviii. 21.   [i] Deut. 16. 21.

SERMON III. 59

worſhip was not neceſſary; the fruits of the earth, and the firſtlings of the flock, were heaped upon the rude and ſimple altar, which the tribe or the family conſecrated to that pious uſe in the vicinity of their camp: thither the devout believer repaired to conſult, as appears to have been the caſe, the oracle of God in caſes of difficulty, to offer up thankſgivings for mercies and benefits received, and to pour forth prayers for future happineſs.

But in after times a numerous multitude, devoted to ſenſible objects, pleaſed with the falſe worſhip of the country which they had quitted, and in that in which they were afterwards ſettled, ſurrounded by nations who delighted in ſhew and pageantry, and all the external glare of ſymbolical worſhip; a people ſo circumſtanced required ſomething more ornamental than the primitive ſimplicity of their forefathers, to ſecure them from the allurements of falſe religion, and to attach them to the naked purity of truth.

God therefore in his mercy, allowing
for

for their natural weakness, and wishing that the awful truth of his Godhead might be firmly rooted in their minds, that they might be without excuse if they looked elsewhere for protection, and offered up to others the homage due only to their God, in consideration to their infirmities gave them visible tokens of his continual presence amongst them. Here it was that the patience and long suffering of God displayed themselves in the most striking manner, by every possible accommodation to their inclinations and their prejudices, nay, I may say, even to their capricious partialities.

It was not enough that the great truth of the unity of the Godhead was formally announced in the presence of the assembled congregation, and that the adoration of strange Gods was expressly forbid; in addition to the positive command, and the positive prohibition, other means were tried to guard the chosen race from the pollutions of idolatry.

To their great progenitor the Almighty had

had announced himself as the God of his family, and to his descendants afterwards, as the tutelary God of the nation. Whilst the nations of Canaan are erecting altars to the Gods of their own creation, the Gods of the hills, as they were called, and the Gods of the valleys, the Holy One of Israel, in compliance with the prevailing prejudices, assumes a name: "Tell them," says he, when he invests his chosen servant with his high commission, " Tell them, that I AM hath sent me unto you [k]."

In the wilderness the tent of Moses was distinguished by the appearance of Divine glory before it. Afterwards the chosen servant of the Almighty was commanded to erect a splendid tabernacle from the pattern which he saw exhibited on the mount; in this tabernacle was placed the ark of the covenant, and here the glory of the Lord resided; the Holy One of Israel sat between the cherubims [l]: from hence the oracles of God were uttered; and before this residence of the Most High, the high Priest appeared annually on the great

[k] Exod. iii. 14.
[l] 2 Sam. vi. 2. 2 Kings xix. 15. Psalm xcix. 1.

day of expiation, when he was to mediate for the sins of all the people.

When the nation had advanced in its conquest of the promised land, this holy tabernacle was fixed at Shiloh; and when the conquest was complete, as far at least as God intended that it should be carried, at that splendid period of their prosperity, when "there was peace in all the land, and every man sat under his vine, and under his fig-tree [m]," the mercy-seat was removed to the city of Jerusalem, and was placed in the house of God with all the pomp and decoration of oriental magnificence.

From the earliest times therefore they were never without the actual presence of God dwelling amongst them; the external symbols of this presence increased in splendor with their national prosperity; and when they themselves were at the zenith of their power, the Temple of their God was the glory of the world.

[m] 1 Kings iv. 25.

SERMON III.

As the Almighty, though a pure Spirit, and to be adored in spirit and in truth, disdained not to reside, and to be worshipped, in a temple made with hands; so also, from the same principle of heavenly benevolence, he prescribed the order and the offices of the priesthood, who were to attend continually upon his service; their offerings, their employments, nay, even the very minute detail of their dresses, and their ordinary life.

I mean not at present to enter into a minute examination of the ceremonial Law; at a future time I shall attempt to explain the figurative nature of this Law, and to shew that, under the wisest of its ordinances, many of the mysterious and awful truths of Christianity were obscurely pourtrayed: but at present I have only to urge, that its high solemnities and splendid festivals contributed to assist the great purpose of separation, by gratifying the fondness of the people for external shew, and presenting continually to their minds the power and the goodness of their own God.

The

The sabbath itself, the earliest and most sacred of their religious institutions, was a continual memorial of the creation, reminding them, as often as it returned, of that day on which the Almighty had rested from all his works, and saw that they were good. The Paschal supper reminded them of their deliverance, when the angel of the Lord smote the Egyptian, and spared the Israelite. The feast of Tabernacles recalled to their recollection their long and severe trials in the wilderness, when every moment of their existence was in fact a testimony of the power of God, and of his Providence watching over their safety; and the feast of Pentecost was a perpetual record of the promulgation of their Law from Mount Sinai, of the ministry of angels, the thunderings and lightnings, and all the mighty signs and wonders which accompanied the fearful presence of their God.

Thus it was wisely and providentially contrived, that the most public and solemn acts of their Religion should perpetuate the memory of the most striking occurrences in in their history; and upon all those occasions it was usual to fix the impression still deeper in the minds of the people, by a summary recapitulation of all which had been done for them, and all the signal acts which, by the Providence of God, they had atchieved; and this was done with all the glow and the ardour of poetical enthusiasm; in songs of triumph for deliverance and victory, and hymns of gratitude for quiet and peaceable possession of the promised land.

Whilst the solemn preparation, and the splendid exhibition of these stated festivals, attached the people to their religion, they also answered the important purpose of attaching them to the country of their inheritance: what was the particular use of increasing this, and of confining all their hopes and all their wishes to their possessions in the land of Canaan, will be seen hereafter; at present I am only concerned to prove the fact.

From the original promise made to Abraham, the inheritance of the land of Canaan

Canaan had been at all times the great object of the wishes of his posterity, and the point to which all their views were directed. A period of more than four centuries of servitude and oppression in Egypt had not obliterated the remembrance of the promise, nor lessened the fond expectation of its accomplishment. At the first summons they were ready to put themselves under the guidance of a leader, who undertook to conduct them to the haven of their wishes; and the wanderings of forty years in dreary and inhospitable desarts, although they tempted them often to murmur and repine, to rebel against the authority of their conductor, and even to accuse the most High God of injustice, yet still they could not extinguish, nay, they even increased, the ardent longing for the possession of that happy land, which was to repay them for all their suffering.

It was natural, therefore, when they at last possessed this expected country, when they found it to be fertile and rich beyond their hopes, " a land of wheat and barley,

ley, and vines, and fig trees, and pomegranates, a land of oil-olive and honey[n]," it was natural that they should love and cherish it with the most partial attachment; but this attachment the wisdom of God augmented and confirmed.

In the first place their religion was local; it was fixed solely to Jerusalem; and the great duties of it could be no where else performed, so that as often as the stated season of their festival returned, all Jews, of whatever description, or wherever their residence might be, were to go up to the holy city to celebrate their festivals; the law was absolute, and of indispensable obligation.

In addition to this obligation there was another law, sanctified indeed by a religious ceremony, but in itself of a nature purely civil: it was impossible for an Israelite to alienate his property; the original allotment was to remain unalterable; and whatever changes or variations might be made, they were constantly to be rec-

[n] Deut. viii. 8.

tified

tified at the feaſt of Jubilee; "for then," ſays the law, "ye ſhall return every man unto his poſſeſſion °."

It is eaſy to ſee the conſequences of this right of redemption; that while the nation at large was preſerved one and entire, each tribe ſeparately, and each family, were careful to preſerve their own records, to aſcertain their own rights, and to claim their own property; a point of material importance in the diſpenſations of Providence. Bethlehem Ephratah thus remained in the portion of Judah, and the lineage of Jeſſe was preſerved to the days of the Meſſiah pure and unmixed, and ſeparate from the genealogy of every other family in Judea.

The great principle of ſeparation was thus purſued within the general outline of the whole community, through all the ſubordinate diviſions, and all the inferior claſſes of ſociety; and whilſt the nation was diſtinguiſhed as a peculiar people from all other people, every tribe and every fa-

° Deut. iii. 20.

mily had some appropriate character, and some peculiar privileges, by which they were separated and discriminated from one another.

If, from their public institutions, and the greater ceremonies of their Religion, we turn our eyes to their ordinary occupations, and the habits of common life, we shall see throughout the marks of the same design, and the effects of the same principle of discrimination.

From the moment of his birth the Jew was marked as a being distinct from the rest of mankind: the initiatory rite of circumcision first stamped him as the servant of God, and admitted him to the privileges of the Patriarchal covenant. As his reason opened, he was educated, not in the rudiments of human science, but in the precepts of Divine wisdom; the holy volume of the Law was opened before him; on that he was told to meditate day and night, " to talk of it when he sat in his house, and when he walked by the way; to bind it for a sign upon his hands, and

and a frontlet between his eyes; to write it upon the posts of his house, and upon his gates ᵖ."

In his Law he found a provision, not only for the higher moralities, and the more important duties, upon which the very existence of civil society depends, but for all the minute occurrences of common life, and all the accidental circumstances which human legislators pass by without notice, because they either consider them as matters of indifference, or do not foresee that they will happen.

For the fashion of his dress, his diet, and the construction of his dwelling, the Jew found in the volumes of his Law, certain and precise regulations; and if he went forth to the labour of the field, the cattle he was to use in his tillage, the seed he was to sow, and the time and mode of gathering his harvest into his garners, were all the subjects of particular and appropriate laws.

ᵖ Deut. vi. 7—9.

SERMON III.

By such apparently trivial means did the Almighty wisdom contrive to fix upon his people a peculiar and discriminate character. For every action of their lives there was a rule prescribed, which limited the particular bias and inclination of his mind; and it was not matter of choice whether they should follow this rule or not; it was indispensably necessary; and punishment instantly followed the violation of it, unless by the atonement of his offerings and sacrifices, the offender could appease the anger of God.

In all ages, and under every variety of situation, of knowledge, of power, or of depression, man must, in the essential characteristics of his nature, be still the same; his passions, and his affections, however modified by circumstances, in their origin and their principles were precisely similar: but climate will sometimes give them a physical alteration, and education and custom a moral habitude. But in no people that ever existed in the world do we see the effects of law and custom marked in such

such strong and legible characters, as in the people of Israel.

Apud ipsos fides obstinata, sed adversus omnes alios hostile odium [q], was the well known censure of Tacitus. But we need not go to the historians or the satirists of Rome, who despised and hated them, for a picture of their defects; out of the mouth of their own countrymen we may condemn them; their sullen pride, their determined obstinacy, and their bigotry, are the continual topics of censure and animated invectives, in all their Historians and all their Prophets; and in later times, the holy Apostle, who knew them well, declares, " that they pleased not God, and were contrary to all men [r]."

If we advert to the spirit, nay, even to the letter of the Mosaic Law, though all communion with idolaters was cut off, there was nothing that could be construed into an approbation of want of friendship, or want of hospitality; nothing certainly that justifies enmity or hatred to the rest

[q] Tacit.   [r] 1 Thess. ii. 15.

SERMON III. 73

of mankind. Let him forsake the worship of strange Gods, and the stranger that sojourned in the land[s] was to be loved and cherished, as well as the descendant from the stock of Abraham; communion of Religion and religious privileges were denied to none; and the proselyte of righteousness, if he submitted to the conditions of the covenant, became to all intents and purposes an Israelite, and was admitted to a participation of all the privileges of the nation.

But still the real descendants of the Patriarch cherished in their own minds a fancied superiority over the convert, whoever he might be; the promises made to their ancestors continually sounded in their ears; that his name would be great, " that he would be a blessing and a great nation;" " that God would bless them that blessed him, and curse them that cursed him;" " that nations and kings would come from him;" and that " in his seed all nations would be blessed[t]." As these promises they

[s] Levit. xvii. 33. xxv. 35. Numb. xv. 14.
[t] Gen. xii. 2.

con-

considered to be the basis of their national establishment, as they had been accomplished in part, by the rapid conquest and secure possession of the land of Canaan, and as all their great leaders, and all their holy Prophets had taught them to attribute their successes to the original covenant, they vainly and foolishly supposed that they should be the lords of the universe, and that every nation under heaven would in time bow down before them.

From this false and mistaken interpretation of the original promise, we may derive the pride and the self-conceit which tempted the Israelites to look down upon the rest of mankind, as a race inferior to themselves; and this national vanity was stimulated and encouraged by fomenting the rivalship and jealousy of the neighbouring nations; of the Moabites, the Ammonites, and the Edomites, who still contended for the birth-right of which their ancestors had been defrauded; and the sons of Ishmael, who never forgot the stock from which they sprang, or the rewards which were annexed to the obedience

dience of their great progenitor. It must be remembered too, that these nations, although connected with the Jews by ties of blood, were marked by a particular exclusion from the favoured church—that, in the case of the Moabites, three generations were to pass away, and in the case of the Edomites, ten, before they could be admitted to the privileges of a proselyte.

On these principles we may account for the pride and the bigotry of the Jewish people; and if it be true, that the human mind naturally attaches itself most to that which is continually before it, and that habit endears to us whatever is frequently repeated; there may be justice in the remark, that their tenacious obstinacy arose from the burthensome nature of their ritual, and the continual repetition of its ceremonies.

But even the vices and the faults in their character, which arose perhaps from their mistaking the object of their institutions, aided the designs of Providence, by keeping up the great national distinction,
till

till the end of the feparation was attained: but at the fame time they deluded the unfortunate people, and taught them to expect permanency and immutability in that which was intended to anfwer a temporary purpofe.

That in the days of our Saviour, when their Temple was ftill ftanding, and their ceremonial Law in full force, when even our Lord himfelf conformed to its cuftoms, and its ceremonies—that the Jews of that time fhould have argued from the expreffions of their Legiflator, that their Law would be everlafting, may not perhaps be thought fo wonderful: but what has a modern Jew to urge, as a reafon for his obftinate adherence to the inftitutions of Mofes?

Chriftian writers have again and again unanfwerably proved from the ufage of the Hebrew language, and the general analogy of all languages, that when the perpetuity of the Mofaic Law is fpoken of, the expreffions can only mean that it fhould laft for a long time, as long as the nature

SERMON III. 77

nature and defign of the inftitution would allow: indeed, if Canaan was given to the people of Ifrael for an " everlafting poffeffion," and they have long ceafed to poffefs it, it is abfurd to infer that the Law was to be of perpetual obligation, becaufe it is faid, that it fhould endure for ever.

But I would afk the modern Jew in the firft inftance, What was the great object of the ceremonial Law? To feparate the people, he will fay, from communication with idolaters, and to leave the worfhip of the true God undefiled. Doubtlefs it was fo; the ftrange deviations of mankind from the truths revealed to the Patriarchs, made it neceffary.

" The Law was added," fays the Apoftle, " becaufe of tranfgreffions[u]." This being acknowledged, what is its ufe when idolatry has ceafed, when the found of the Heathen oracles has long been hufhed, the ftatues of their corrupt Deities have been crumbled to the duft, and all the ci-

[u] Galat. iii. 19.

vilized

vilized nations of the world unite in the adoration of the one true God?

Then I would afk him, whether in their Law, which he afferts to be immutable, there were not actually changes made, as the time approached at which the obligation was to ceafe, and all its partial diftinctions to be done away?

Before the building of the fecond Temple, God enlarged the boundaries of his church; he admitted into its communion thofe whom legal impediments or natural diftinctions had before excluded from it. "My falvation," fays the Holy Spirit, "is near to come, and my righteoufnefs to be revealed [x]. Let not the fon of the ftranger fay, The Lord hath utterly feparated me from his people; neither let the eunuch fay, Behold, I am a dry tree [y]; for even unto thee will I give in mine houfe, and within my walls, a place and a name better than of fons and of daughters; I will give them an everlafting name, that fhall not be cut off [z]."

[x] Ifaiah lvi. 1.   [y] Ifaiah lvi. 3.   [z] Ifaiah lvi. 5.

SERMON III.

At the fame time a change was announced in the mode of God's government; for the iniquities of the fathers were no more to be punifhed upon the children, but every one was to bear his own fins: it was alfo declared, that the external and pofitive duties of facrifice and oblations were inferior to the inward and unbidden worfhip of the heart, and that "God defired mercy and not facrifice[a]," and the knowledge of God more than burnt offering.

If thefe material alterations are not fufficient to prove that the whole was a preparatory difpenfation, and confequently might ceafe when its object was accomplifhed; let him advert to the circumftances of his people; they no longer dwell alone, but are fcattered abroad over the face of the earth; they are no longer the "habitation of the Lord;" nor do they dwell in fafety under "his everlafting arms[b];" all the diftinctions, which would now be ufelefs, are gone; the genealogies, which they once preferved with fuch anxious care, are

[a] Hofea vi. 6.   [b] Deut. xxxiii. 27.

confounded with each other, and the tribe of Judah is mingled and lost in the common mass of their countrymen [c].

Thus their temporal and their spiritual state, which were in fact one and the same thing, which gradually rose together to the height of their fame and splendour, were both destroyed when the purpose of their establishment was fulfilled.

Lastly, let him recollect, that the whole of his worship, as I have before remarked, was local; that all its duties were to be performed at Jerusalem, and no where else. If then the holy country be trodden under foot by aliens and strangers; if the holy Temple be destroyed; if all traces of its existence have long been gone, and all attempts to restore it have proved fruitless and abortive; is it not time for him to confess that the hour is really arrived, when " God is not to be worshipped on mount Gerizim [d], or at Jerusalem," but in the hearts of all his creatures?

[c] Newton on the Prophecies, vol i. p. 215.
[d] Judges ix. 7. John xxi. 21.

# SERMON IV.

COLOSSIANS ii. 17.

WHICH ARE A SHADOW OF GOOD THINGS TO COME, BUT THE BODY IS OF CHRIST.

HAVING already explained for what purpose the Almighty separated the Jewish nation from the rest of mankind, and by what methods that separation was effected, the course of my argument leads me to examine what sort of connexion there was between the religious institutions of the Jews, and the essential doctrines of Christianity; and in what sense, and under what limitations, the former are

are to be considered as Figures and Types of the latter.

The Apostle in this Epistle to the Colossians takes great pains to caution the Jewish converts against a practice, in those days very common, of mixing and uniting the complicated ritual of Moses with the spiritual precepts and the simpler sacraments of Christ. He tells them, that the Gospel into which they had been baptized was all in all; that it contained " all the treasures of wisdom and knowledge;" that they were " complete in Christ," in whom dwelt all the fulness of the Godhead bodily[a]; and that as they were not to be seduced by the false theories of Greek and Oriental philosophy, so they were to pay no heed to the bigoted Israelite, when he attempted to impose upon them the burthensome yoke of useless ceremonies; of laws which Christ had abrogated, and of rites, which, as they were nothing more than images and shadows of the truth, consequently were of no avail to those who possessed the reality and the substance.

[a] Col. ii. 9.

SERMON IV. 83

stance. "Let no man judge you," says he, "in meat, or drink, or in respect of an holy day, or the new moon, or of sabbaths, which are a shadow of things to come, but the body is of Christ [b]."

The Apostolic Epistles abound with expressions of a similar tendency. The priests under the Law are said "to serve unto the shadow of heavenly things [c];" the Law itself is said to have "a shadow of good things to come, and not the very image of the things [d];" the tabernacle and its decorations are called the patterns or copies, ὑποδείγματα, of heavenly things; and Christ is declared to have entered not "into the holy places made with hands, which are the Figures or Antitypes of the true, but into heaven itself [e]."

Now when the Apostles make use of such expressions as these, when they style the Law of Moses, or rather the Levitical part of the Mosaic Law, a shadow, a figure, or a type of future good things, and

[b] Col. ii. 16.   [c] Heb. ii. 5.
[d] Heb. x. 1.   [e] Heb. ix. 24.

Christ the body, the substance, and the truth, do they mean merely to urge the superiority of Christianity over Judaism, of the Gospel over the Law, and the sacrifice of Jesus over the stated sacrifices of the Aaronic priesthood? Or do they mean, that the ordinances of the Mosaic dispensation were designed by God to prefigure future events in the history of our Saviour, and to represent, under the shade of allegory, those mysterious truths of his religion which were not to be revealed till the " fulness of time" arrived?

In the very infancy of Christianity the Commentators of the Gospel began to indulge themselves in the licence of allegorical and mystical interpretations. The Jews in their Targums (which almost superseded the use of the original books of the Law) had long been in the habit of accommodating the obscurities of their Scriptures to their own visionary notions; of drawing parallels, which in all probability never were designed; and of discovering similitudes, which at all times it is easy to to trace in the analogous operations of nature, and still easier to imagine where they do not exist; and, after their example, some of the Greek Fathers gave the reins to their imaginations, and wandered far away from the obvious and literal meaning of Scripture phraseology.

From hence it has happened, that whilst infidel writers have blasphemed the word of God, as if it contained nothing but doubtful phrases, and unsubstantial allegories, upon which no certain dependance could be placed, believers of cool and temperate judgments have been fearful of admitting any figurative interpretations whatever, and have tenaciously adhered to the literal meaning of a text, even where it seems clearly to have been inserted by the Holy Spirit for the sake of the application to be made of it in later times.

In this, as in all other cases, the truth lies between the two extremes; and it is of material importance, that we may not either abuse or reject any portion of the light which God hath mercifully given us, to ascertain,

certain, as accurately as can be done in a cafe of great nicety, what types really are, upon what grounds it is that they have a place in the preparatory difpenfation of the Jews, and what degree of force they may fairly and juftly be allowed to have as evidences of the truth of Chriftianity.

In its primitive and original meaning, a type is merely the pattern, or impreffion, the rough draught, or fketch, from which a more perfect work is made: in this fenfe the word is ufed by the facred writers. Our tranflators have given a variety of interpretations of the Greek word τύπος: in St. John's Gofpel it is rendered by the word Print; "Except I fhall fee in his hands the print of the nails, and put my finger into the print of the nails, I will not believe [f]:" in the Acts of the Apoftles it is tranflated a Figure, or Model: in St. Paul's Epiftle to the Romans, the term Form is ufed—"That form of doctrine which was delivered to you [g]:" and in the courfe of the Apoftolical Epiftles it is continually tranflated, Example; "Now all thefe things

[f] John xx. 25.   [g] Rom. vi. 17.

hap-

SERMON IV. 87

happened unto them for examples[h];" "Now thefe things were our examples[i];" and "Mark them which walk fo as ye have us for an example[k]."

It is evident, that in all thefe paffages, though the expreffion varies, the fame idea of a Pattern, a Copy, of fomething to be copied or imitated, is ftill preferved; and no clearer notion can be formed of the connexion which fubfifts between the Type and its Antitype, than by comparing it with the fimilitude, which may be traced between the firft general delineation of a picture, and the picture completely finifhed[l]."

The language of the firft fimple ages of mankind was neceffarily very imperfect and defective. Time and Experience and Philofophy have taught us to exprefs in words every poffible combination of human thought, and all the varieties of human affections and paffions: but it was not fo with the primitive ages. As yet unaccuftomed to reflect, to abftract and

---

[h] 1 Cor. v. 7.   [i] 1 Cor. x. 6.   [k] Phil. iii. 17.
[l] Jortin's Remarks on Ecclefiaftical Hiftory, vol. i.

to generalize their ideas, they had nothing to reprefent by their fymbols of fpeech, but the common neceffities, and the ordinary employments of life; and when any thing farther was requifite, when they had occafion to fpeak of any thing out of the beaten track of their ufual wants and occupations, it was not to be done by words, but by fome material fign, fome fenfible image taken from the objects that immediately furrounded them: thus arofe a mode of communication by figns or by action, which amply fupplied the deficiencies of language, and enabled mankind, in the earlieft periods of fociety, to communicate to each other thofe ideas for which as yet they had invented no fignificant words.

This fpecies of language was coeval with the origin of mankind; its ufe is founded in nature, and in the natural wants of man: but in procefs of time, what was originally dictated by neceffity, was preferved by choice, was embodied into a regular fyftem, and guided by fixed rules and determinate principles.

When-

SERMON IV. 89

Whenever the Almighty vouchsafes to deliver his instructions to mankind, the mode in which they are delivered is always mercifully accommodated to the character of the people who are to receive them—to their popular opinions, to their customs, and their circumstances: for this reason it is that the inspired writings, both of the Old and New Testament, abound in every page with that method of communicating information by external signs, and sensible representations, to which the Jews had long been attached by inclination, and familiarized by habit.

It frequently happened, that when the Prophet wished to impress more forcibly upon the minds of his hearers the expectation of some approaching event, he drew his parable, or his sign, from the surrounding objects, precisely in the same way that our blessed Lord himself was accustomed to enforce his holy lessons, by a fable, or an allegory, framed from the circumstances of the moment, from the time of the year, from the place in which he was, or from the characters and the employments of the

persons

persons to whom he was speaking. Thus it was that the holy Samuel signified to Saul by the rent in his garment, that the kingdom of Israel would in that day be torn from him[m]; and thus the Prophet Isaiah, by an allusion to the Sabbatic year, exemplified to Hezekiah the conquest of the Jews by Sennacherib, and their subsequent return to Jerusalem[n]. Sometimes the Prophet himself in his own person acted the event which the Spirit of God empowered him to foresee; thus, by breaking in pieces a potter's vessel, Jeremiah prefigured to the Jews the utter destruction of their city[o]—by putting on yokes and fetters, he foretold to the princes of Edom, Moab, and Ammon, their future defeat, and their subjection to the king of Babylon[p]—by binding the book of his Prophecy to a stone, and casting them both into the Euphrates, he announced that Babylon should sink, and never rise from the evil that was to be brought upon her[q]. In the same manner the Prophet Isaiah, by the name which he gives to his child, fore-

[m] 1 Sam. xv. 27.   [n] Isai. xxxvii. 30.   [o] Jer. xix.
[p] Jer. xxvii.   [q] Jer. li.

SERMON IV. 91

tels, that the riches of Damascus and the spoil of Samaria shall be seized by the Assyrians [r]. And Ezekiel, by going forth in the dress, and with the trembling action of a captive, exemplified the conquest of Zedekiah, and the slavery of his people in Babylon [s].

Such were the methods by which the Prophets of God instructed their countrymen. But it sometimes happened, that the Holy Spirit, in compliance with the common and familiar usage of the Jewish people, adopted the same method of conveying its revelations to the Prophet himself. Thus, for instance, the Prophet Jeremiah is ordered to behold " the rod of the almond-tree, and the seething-pot [t];" and to the Prophet Ezekiel is shewn " the resurrection of the dry bones [u]."

It is needless to multiply instances; they are to be found in every part of the Prophetical books; and, it is evident, that wherever they occur, there is always the

[r] Isai. viii. 3, 4.
[t] Jer. i. 11. 13.
[s] Ezek. xii. 8.
[u] Ezek. xxxvii.

notion

notion of futurity, something is represented that is to happen at a greater or less distance of time; and this is the essential character of a type, and constitutes the difference between the type and the symbol. A Horn, for instance, in the language of Scripture, denotes strength; " an Eye, or a Sceptre," majesty; the Planets, empires and states: but in these emblematic representations there is no idea of futurity, or of future events implied, consequently they are not types, but symbols.

So far then we have considered the general character of types, and the use which the Prophets frequently made of them, to prefigure to the Jews the vicissitudes which took place from time to time in their temporal circumstances: from thence it is easy to proceed to those actions or those ceremonies in the œconomy of Judaism, which we suppose to have been preparatory representations of Christ and his Gospel.

Christian writers have divided these types into three classes, 1st, the remarkable events in the history of the Jewish people; 2dly, the

the characters of illustrious persons, Patriarchs, Kings, or Conquerors; and 3dly, the rites and ceremonies of their Religion. But it is absolutely necessary, that we may not be lost in the labyrinth of fanciful analogies and absurd comparisons, which are the delight of fanatics and enthusiasts, to fix some determinate boundary, some certain criterion, by which we can estimate the real value of an argument, drawn from typical analogy: and what can this criterion be, but the authority of inspiration? Admitting then that other similitudes, and other parallelisms, may have the appearance of reason, and may perhaps be just, we cannot surely be wrong in refusing to acknowledge any circumstance in the Old Testament to be a shadow or token of Christ, unless the writers of the New Testament have declared it to be so.

In the Jewish history doubtless there is a striking analogy, an analogy pointed out and illustrated by the Apostles themselves, between many of the most miraculous events, and the general state of mankind, and their particular situation under the
Gospel

Gospel covenant; between their servitude in Egypt for instance, and the tyranny of sin; between their baptism in the sea and in the cloud, and the baptismal rite of Christianity; between their sufferings during their passage through the wilderness, and the temptations, trials, and difficulties of the present world; between the Sabbath of rest promised to them in the temporal possession of Canaan, and the eternal rest to be enjoyed hereafter in Heaven: in all these circumstances there is an analogy and a correspondence, which we cannot well suppose to have taken place accidentally, or without the design and determined purpose of the Almighty.

It was at all times the delight of the Jewish people, to trace resemblances between the most distinguished of their countrymen and the glorious Messiah, who, in the latter age of the world, was to conduct them to power and preeminence above the rest of mankind. But these resemblances, with whatever ingenuity they may be discovered, or to whatever degree of minuteness they may be carried, want, for the most

most part, the necessary sanction of inspiration. The father indeed of the human race is declared by the Apostle to be the "figure of him who was to come[x]:" but of the rest, of Joseph, Sampson, or Joshua, no such declaration is made; and although it must be allowed, that there is a striking similitude between the events of their lives, and the character, office, and circumstances of the Messiah, yet we cannot venture to pronounce, that the former were designed to represent or prefigure the latter.

But if we go on from historical facts and distinguished persons, to the Ceremonies of the Jewish Law, the similitudes become more obvious and more satisfactory.

The ceremonial Precepts of the Mosaic Law relate either to the worship of God, and the daily service of the Temple; or to the persons of the people, and their conduct in life. Of the latter, the principal object was, as we have seen upon a former

[x] Rom. v. 14.

occasion,

occasion, by a distinction of dress, of diet, and of occupation, to keep up the great separation, " the partition-wall," between the people of Israel and the nations who surrounded them. Whether besides this object, under the covert of ablutions and purifications, it was not designed to enforce the necessity of inward purity and moral virtue, is a question foreign to our present discussion, which must be confined merely to the ritual of their worship.

The Temple at Jerusalem was a copy of that Tabernacle which Moses built by the command of God in the Wilderness, from the heavenly model exhibited to him in the mount. In the outer part, the Priests performed the daily functions of their ministry; but into the holy Sanctuary, which the Jews considered as a symbol of heaven, the High Priest went alone, annually, with blood to atone for the sins of the people—a circumstance designed, it should seem, to prefigure the one oblation and satisfaction to be made by Christ, who, after his death, was to reascend to the glory which he had with the Father before the worlds.

It

SERMON IV.

It can scarcely be supposed, that the striking similitude between the sacrifice of the Paschal Lamb and the sacrifice of our Redeemer was accidental: let us attend to the circumstances. Christ was slain on the same day that the Paschal Lamb was; no bones of either were broken; as the Lamb was without spot or blemish, so was Christ without sin: and as the blood of the Lamb sprinkled on the door-posts was a token and memorial of deliverance from the slaughter of the first-born; so the blood of Christ purchased for us a spiritual deliverance from the thraldom of sin and iniquity.

But if this resemblance between the Passover and the death of our Lord be far the most striking that can be produced, it is equally certain, however, that all the legal sacrifices, whether they were completed within or without the camp, whether they were offered as an atonement for the sins of the community at large, on the great day of expiation; or for the sins of particular families or individuals, upon the commission of the offence; insomuch as they contained
the

the principle of expiation, and atonement, and redemption from sin, they all represented the future death of Christ; and upon this account it may not appear perhaps so extravagant an expression as has been supposed, to assert, that the Gospel is contained in the Law; for the ceremonial part of the Mosaic Law was, in fact, a constant allusion to the Gospel; and there is no reason, *primâ facie*, why it should not be so: on the contrary, there is every reason from the nature of the case to suppose, that a dispensation, which was a preparation and rudiment for a better and more perfect system to come, would contain in its institutions, frequent tokens and indications to that future system.

Christianity and Judaism, it must ever be remembered, are not independent, unconnected systems of Religion, but mutually dependent on each other, as parts of the same general scheme of Providence, for the happiness of man. Successive Revelations, if they are really Divine, must be necessarily successive discoveries of truth; consequently they cannot contradict each other, they

they cannot be inconsistent with each other. But in the gradual communication of truth, what is at first seen faintly and obscurely, will, in process of time, become gradually clearer, till at length the day-spring from on high breaks forth upon us in all its lustre.

God hath vouchsafed, at different times, to make two covenants with his creatures: the one carnal, sanctioned by temporal promises, and enjoining the performance of a multitude of external ordinances; the other spiritual, applying to the heart and understanding, and raising our thoughts beyond the frivolous concerns of our present transitory existence, to the enjoyment of a boundless eternity. But however different they might be in form, in institution, and in ceremonies, in substance the two covenants are the same; the great design of both was the same; the Mediator of both was the same; and the vital principle of both, faith in the power and the promises of God.

To redeem mankind from the punishment of death which they had incurred, and to restore them to immortality, was the one great scheme of Providence; for this gracious purpose, Christ was to suffer death upon the cross. The time at which this awful event was to happen, and the steps which were gradually to lead to its accomplishment, were all fixed by God, long before the ratification of the first covenant, before even the act of creation itself. So the Apostles speak of the great mystery of Christianity: " The wisdom of God," says St. Paul, " is a mystery, even the hidden wisdom which God ordained before the world to our glory [y];" and " ye are not redeemed with corruptible things," says St. Peter, " but with the precious blood of Christ, who was pre-ordained before the foundation of the world [z]." So also St. John says, that " the Lamb of God was slain from the foundation of the world [a]."

That the holy Jesus therefore should make an atonement for the sins of mankind, by a voluntary oblation of himself upon the cross, was from all eternity the

[y] 1 Cor. ii. 7. [z] 1 Pet. i. 18. 20. [a] Rev. xiii. 8.

purpose

purpose of Almighty wisdom. In the Divine mind, the whole mysterious scheme extending throughout all ages, from the very commencement of time to the final consummation of all things, was comprehended under one point of view, as one complete and perfect plan. " Known unto God are all his works from the beginning [b]." To man, the dispensations of God present themselves in detached parts, and with different degrees of clearness or obscurity; and even now we comprehend them imperfectly. To God there can be no varieties of knowledge, and no gradations of time.

But though the certain knowledge of this precious sacrifice was reserved for the latter days, it was at all times operating continually to produce the blessed effects of Sanctification and Redemption. The righteous Patriarchs before the promulgation of the Law, and all holy and religious men under the Law, were justified, as we are, by the free gift of God, through the mediation of Christ. " Abraham [c]," they are the words of our Saviour himself, " Abra-

[b] Acts xv. 18. [c] John viii. 56.

ham rejoiced to see the day of Chrift;" and we with reafon fuppofe, that he faw it typically in the intended facrifice of his own fon. " He believed," we are told, " and his faith was counted unto him for righteoufnefs ᵈ." St. Paul tells the Corinthians, that " the Fathers were all under the cloud, and were baptized in the fea, and did eat the fame fpiritual meat, and drank of the fpiritual Rock," following them, " and that Rock was Chrift ᵉ."

The Fathers therefore were all juftified, not by their own works, or by their own righteoufnefs, but by the all-fufficient merits of the facrifice of Jefus Chrift, " the fame yefterday, and to-day, and for ever ᶠ."

In what way the future death of the Redeemer could operate, fo as to fave thofe who died before he came into the world, it is prefumptuous in man to inquire; it is amongft the deep and hidden counfels of the Almighty: it is enough for us that it did fo; and it is certainly confiftent with our notions of the goodnefs of God, to fuppofe that it would do fo; that faith, under every

ᵈ Gen. xv. 6.   ᵉ 1 Cor. x. 1—4.   ᶠ Heb. xiii. 8.

dif-

dispensation, would operate unto salvation; and that at all times a repentant sinner would receive pardon and remission of sins, provided that he performed the sacrificatory rites, and complied with the acts of obedience which the dispensation under which he lived, and the state of his knowledge, enabled him to perform; " for every law doth speak to those which live under it."

And this being the case, it is unquestionably consistent with the usual method which God takes to instruct mankind, that ceremonies which were only to be temporary, and sacrifices which were only to atone partially for the sins of a particular people, and in that people only for sins of a particular description, should, in their form and all external circumstances, represent the great and final sacrifice, whose efficacy was to be universal and endure to the end of time.

That God should thus foreshew to his chosen people those truths which it was not possible at the time fully to reveal to them by a mode of instruction familiar to their con-

conceptions, and adapted to their capacities, by material reprcfentations, is no more difficult to conceive, than that he fhould impower his Prophets to reprefent the future glories of Chrift's kingdom, by expreffions and defcriptions taken from the fertility, the opulence, and the fplendor of their temporal poffeffions; or that he fhould compel them, by the impulfe of his Holy Spirit, to anticipate the triumphs of the Meffiah, and the univerfal extent of his dominion, when perhaps they imagined themfelves, that they were merely celebrating the triumphs and the profperity of David, or Solomon, or Zerubbabel.

If fuch then be the nature of types in general, and fuch the principle upon which it is reafonable to fuppofe that they would have a place in the general œconomy of the Divine difpenfations, it only remains for us to confider, how far we may juftly reafon from them, and in what way they may be produced as evidences of the truth of Chriftianity.

No perfon, I apprehend, would attempt
to

SERMON IV. 105

to make a convert to the Chriftian faith, by typical reafoning; he would argue indeed from Prophecy; he would fhew him whom he wifhed to convince, that the appearance of an extraordinary perfon upon earth had been foretold from the very beginning of the world; that the time of his coming, his character, his office, and his death, had been minutely defcribed. He would tell him that Chrift claimed to be this perfon, and that he fupported his claim by acts of fuperhuman power, and this would amount to proof.

A Prophecy accomplifhed by the event is a proof; a Type is not, however exact the fimilitude may be; and they who attempt to give to types the importance of direct demonftrative proofs, neither underftand their nature nor their real ufe. Did the Jews themfelves, we may afk, ever at any period of their hiftory previous to the birth of Chrift, imagine that their Law and its ordinances were typical reprefentations of their Meffiah, and that the facrifices of the Aaronic priefthood were prophetical reprefentations of the atonement for fin to be made by him?

That

That men of religious minds, who studied their Law with devout hearts, and really wished to discover the will of God, might see and understand the inefficacy of their own sacrifices, cannot be denied: "without shedding of blood they knew there could be no remission of sins[g]" whatever. "Flesh with the life thereof, which is the blood, their ancestors had been forbidden to eat[h];" and in the volume of their Law they were told, that it was death to eat the blood, because God had reserved it for the altar, to make an atonement for their souls. "For it is the blood," says the Law, "that maketh an atonement for the soul[i];" at the same time, even the shedding of blood did not expiate for all sins. The sin-offering and the trespass-offering expiated sins of ignorance, and sins of inferior magnitude: but there were sins for which no such expiation could be made; Idolatry, for instance, and contempt of the Law of Moses: they were to be punished with death without mercy. Upon such occasions, therefore, we can scarcely conceive, but that serious and pious men must have raised their thoughts to some

[g] Heb. ix. 22.   [h] Lev. xvii. 14.   [i] Lev. xvii. 11.

higher

SERMON IV. 107

higher and better atonement, to be granted, as the Holy Psalmist expresses it, " by the loving-kindness of God, and the multitude of his tender mercies[k]."

From their own Prophets too they must have learnt to expect a change in their legal ceremonies, and the introduction of another system, otherwise they must have supposed a strange inconsistency in the word of God. For although God prescribes and regulates the sacrifice, the Holy Spirit is continually expressing displeasure and dislike of it. " To what purpose is the multitude of your sacrifices unto me? I delight not in the blood of bulls, and of lambs, and of he-goats; your new moons and your appointed feasts my soul hateth; they are a trouble to me, I am weary to bear them[l]." The prophet Daniel expresly tells them, that the time would come, when the sacrifice and the oblation should cease[m]. And both Isaiah and Daniel, when they are painting in lofty terms, and splendid imagery, the expected Christ, and the glories of his kingdom, declare, that he

[k] Psalm lxix. 16.   [l] Isa. i. 11—14.   [m] Dan. ix. 27.

will be both the priest and the victim at the same time. And yet the Jews certainly did not conclude from hence, that their Messiah was to die, to atone for their sins, and not only for theirs, but for the sins of the whole world. If, from the opinion of the earlier Jews, we advert to the practice of our blessed Lord himself, and of those inspired persons to whom he committed the care of his infant church, we do not find that they ever insist upon types as direct proofs; that they place them upon a level, for instance, with the two great proofs of the truth of Christianity, the accomplishment of Scriptural prophecy, and the display of miracles. St. Paul in his Epistle to the Hebrew converts (if at least I may be permitted to attribute to that holy Apostle a composition which is stamped with the strongest characters both of his eloquence and his mode of arguing) is drawing throughout a comparison between the Law of Moses and the Gospel of Christ. His object is to persuade the converts to persevere in the faith into which they had been baptized. Some of them had been seduced by the subtle reasoning

of

of Jewish teachers; and the firmness of others had been shaken by distress, and trials, and persecutions: the Apostle therefore is labouring to inspire them with fortitude, by painting on the one part the glorious rewards of unshaken constancy; and on the other, the dangers and the punishments which are reserved for apostacy. With this view he enters into a minute comparison of the two covenants, he points out the circumstances of resemblance and coincidence in each, and deduces from thence the infinite superiority of the Gospel above the Law. The Law was given by the ministry of angels; the Gospel, by the Son of God; the brightness of his glory, and the express image of his person. The ceremonies of the Law were administered to the Jews by a succession of mortal men: the Gospel had one High Priest, even Jesus the Son of God, who was invested with an eternal and unchangeable priesthood; a priesthood resembling not that of Aaron, but of Melchisedeck, who was both a King and the Priest of the most High God. The first covenant had its ordinances, its tabernacle, and its
sanc-

sanctuary; but "Jesus Christ is gone into a better tabernacle, into a temple not made with hands, into heaven itself[n]." Under the Law, the blood of bulls and of goats was shed to atone for transgressions; but Jesus Christ hath offered up himself once for all, and by his own blood hath entered into the holy place, having obtained eternal redemption for us. Who then, is the conclusion of the Apostle, would quit a more excellent and more perfect Religion, to return to one less perfect, and less efficacious? Or if transgression and disobedience under the latter received their just punishment, who can suppose that it is not in the highest degree criminal to reject the salvation offered by the former? In all this comparison which the Apostle makes, which in fact is a comparison between the Type and its Antitype; between the rough draught or shadow of good things to come, and the substance of those very good things; there is nothing like an attempt to prove the truth of the Gospel, from the figurative character of the Law: on the contrary, the Apostle expressly

[n] Heb. ix. 11—24.

calls

calls upon the Hebrews, to leave the principles of the doctrine of Chrift, and to go on unto perfection; not to return again to the elements, to the fundamental arguments, and the neceffary evidences of their faith, which he ftates to be the doctrine of repentance, of faith in God, of baptifm, of the refurrection of the dead, and of the eternal Judgment°. This therefore is the nature of his argument; it was addreffed, we know, to Jews, and to thofe who, having embraced Chriftianity, wifhed to return to Judaifm. You prefer, he would fay, the Law of Mofes to the Gofpel of Chrift; but why do ye fo? For your Law was evidently defective in the one great point of redemption from fin. Could your legal facrifices have atoned effectually for fin, would it have been neceffary to repeat them fo often? Would not one expiation have been fufficient? And then would they not have ceafed to be offered? But your Priefts daily minifter in the Temple, and offer repeatedly the fame facrifices, which can never take away fin; they are only to be looked upon therefore as the fi-

° Heb. vi. 1, 2.

gures

gures or shadows, by which the Holy Ghost signified a more perfect sacrifice to be made hereafter. That sacrifice is made; Jesus Christ hath offered himself without spot unto God for us; he is our Passover, which is sacrificed for us; he is the very Lamb of God, which taketh away the sins of the world, and by one sacrifice he hath perfected for ever them that are sanctified[p].

The doctrine of the Apostle throughout the whole of the Epistle is evidently this, that the sacrifices of the Law were allusions to the great and final atonement to be made by the blood of Christ: and though the Apostle does not tell us so, we may venture to conclude, that the design of God in prefiguring the death of our Saviour by the tokens and shadows of the Law, was to facilitate the promulgation of Christianity, and to prepare the Jewish nation, and through them the whole race of man, for the awful and mysterious doctrines of Sanctification, and Redemption, and adoption to eternal life. Our blessed Redeemer himself, it may be observed, when

[p] Heb. x. 14.

he

SERMON IV.

he is celebrating the laft Pafchal Supper with his difciples, ufes the very form of expreffion which the Jewifh lawgiver was commanded by God to ufe, when he ratified the covenant of the Law. " Drink ye all of this, faid he; for this is my blood of the New Teftament, which is fhed for you for the remiffion of fins[q];" as Mofes, when he took the book of the covenant, fprinkled it with blood, and faid, " This is the blood of the covenant, which the Lord hath made with you[r]." And when a Jew heard that Chrift was an High Prieft, " a propitiatory facrifice," and " the very Lamb of God;" when he was told that "he fuffered for fins," " the juft for the unjuft," that " he gave his life, himfelf a ranfom," that " he redeemed us with his blood," and " by his death deftroyed him that had the power of death;" the ideas raifed in his mind by fuch expreffions were familiar to him; they were the firft and earlieft leffon of his childhood: the conftant habits of his life, his daily employments, and his hourly meditations, indelibly fixed them in his memory; and he

[q] Matt. xxvi. 27. [r] Exod. xxiv. 8.

had, in fact, only to transfer to Chrift and his Gofpel the notions which he had derived from Mofes and his Law.

By the follower of Mofes typical reafoning would be more readily admitted, and more acutely inveftigated, than it would by the Gentile convert; but its real ufe was the fame to both, not as in itfelf a fufficient evidence of the truth of Chriftianity, but as a valuable acceffion to neceffary and fundamental proofs, a confirmation of truths which the mind had already received, and an illuftration of myfterious doctrines, which would otherwife have been perfectly new and ftrange to their conceptions. At the fame time, it muft be remembered, which is in truth the reafon why I have dwelt fo long upon the fubject, that that fort of analogy upon which the ufe of types in the Old Teftament, and their application in the New, depends, is to all men alike, to the Jew or the Gentile, to the convert of the Apoftolic age, or the confirmed Chriftian of our times, a clear and decifive proof of the unity of God's defign; it convinces us, that the

the gracious purpose of man's redemption and restoration to eternal life was never forgotten; that, in every state of religious knowledge, indications of it were given, conformable to the circumstances of the times, and corresponding with the method of instruction then in use; and that whatever ordinances God thought fit to prescribe, either to the Patriarchs before the Law, or their posterity under the Law, " Christ was in fact the end of them all, for righteousness, unto every one that believeth[s]."

[s] Rom. x. 4.

SERMON V.

ACTS x. 43.

TO HIM GIVE ALL THE PROPHETS WITNESS.

IT was the will of God, that the religion, which in his good time was to become univerſal, ſhould be announced to the world long before its actual publication in two ways; figuratively, by the ceremonies of the Moſaical Law; and literally, by the deſcriptions of the holy Prophets, who ſpake as the ſpirit of God directed them.

Of the firſt of theſe two methods of previous repreſentation, I have attempted in my former discourse to explain the true and legitimate use; I now proceed with a more assured step, and less apprehension of error, to point out the origin of the second, and to trace its progress, from its earliest commencement to its cessation in the Jewish Church.

In the addresses of our blessed Lord to the Jews of his days, one of the characters, which he constantly assumes to himself, is this, that he is the person of whom Moses in the Law, and the Prophets, did write: " I that speak unto thee *Am He*[a]," is his own emphatical expression to the woman of Samaria: and when, after his resurrection, he is conversing with the two disciples who knew him not, he speaks of his own actions, and his own sufferings, as being necessary, because they had been foretold; he says, " O fools, and slow of heart to believe all that the Prophets have written! Ought not Christ to have suffered these things, and to enter into his glory[b]?"

The awful scheme of Prophecy, if it be

[a] John iv. 26.   [b] Luke xxiv. 25, 26.

SERMON V.

considered in a general view, not only refers to the coming of Christ in the flesh, and to the introduction and final establishment of Christianity, but includes also in its comprehensive range the fortunes of almost all the kingdoms of the antient world; it is not the rise, or the overthrow, of opulent states and mighty empires alone, of Tyre, of Egypt, or of Babylon, which the Holy Spirit predicts; but with equal precision, and equal certainty, it marks the time, and the manner, in which the inferior kingdoms of Moab, and Edom, of Ammon, and of Amalek, are gradually to yield to the increasing power of their neighbours; and it does so, because all the kingdoms of the ancient world, as they rose successively to power, were implicated in some way or other in the fates and fortunes of the people of Israel, either as the ministers of Almighty vengeance, to punish that people for disobedience and rebellion, or as the agents of his mercy, to rescue them from banishment, and to reinstate them in the possessions of their inheritance.

It seems therefore to have been the design of God, when he poured forth his Holy Spirit upon the Prophets of Israel, in the first instance, to give support and encouragement to his chosen people; to teach them, that even when they thought themselves most neglected, forsaken, and desolate, they were still under the guidance of his paternal arm; that his anger would in time give place to mercy; and that then the cup of his vengeance would be poured out, with full measure, upon the heads of their oppressors. But these gracious assurances had also the higher view of inspiring them with confidence in the power and the promise of their God; that when they saw the temporal prediction literally verified, and the temporal promise actually fulfilled, they might anticipate, without any fear of deception or disappointment, the approach of that great Deliverer, who was to bring with him blessings and salvation " to the whole race of mankind."

The true end of all Prophecy, therefore, was to announce the Redeemer of mankind; and whatever intermediate purposes were

SERMON V.

were to be anfwered; whatever light the omnifcience of God thought fit to throw upon the future fortunes, either of the Jews, or any other nation, it was done with a view ultimately to bear witnefs to the character, office, and fufferings of the bleffed Jefus; and to defcribe the nature of that Religion, which he came into the world to eftablifh.

"To him," faid St. Peter, "give *All* the Prophets witnefs [c]." And upon another occafion, the fame Apoftle tells the Jews, "that Chrift hath fulfilled the things, which God hath fhewed by the mouth of *All* his Prophets [d]." And again, after arguing from the authority of Mofes, he adds, "yea, and all the Prophets from Samuel, and thofe that follow after, as many as have fpoken, have likewife foretold of thefe days [e]." So alfo, our bleffed Lord himfelf, when he wifhed to convince his doubting and incredulous difciples, explained to them his own hiftory, "beginning at Mofes," as the hiftorian informs us, "and *All* the Prophets [f]."

[c] Acts x. 43.
[d] Acts iii. 18.
[e] Acts iii. 24.
[f] Luke xxiv. 27.

From these passages of Holy Writ it may be inferred, that the Prophecies of the Old Testament are not to be considered separately, as so many detached and distinct revelations of God's designs; but as forming a complete and connected system, tending to one and the same important end, and that they are only to be understood by considering them in a regular series, with a view to that end.

That any one accomplished Prophecy is a demonstration of the interposition of God, cannot be disputed; because in any instance to reveal the secrets of futurity, is beyond the reach of human powers. But allowing this to be true, it must be granted also, that the proof of Divine agency will have a stronger effect upon the mind, in proportion to the variety of circumstances predicted; to the distance of time between the Prophecy and its accomplishment; to the strangeness and improbability of the facts revealed, and to the minute delineation of particulars; and of course it will follow, that the mind cannot possibly receive such conviction from any single Prophecy applied to Christ, as from a connected

nected view and comparison of the whole together.

Such a comparison as this, or rather the outline of such a comparison, it is my intention to trace on the present occasion; more than the outline it will be impossible for me to give; and the nature of my subject only calls upon me to shew, that Christianity was foretold by a regular succession of Prophecies, commencing from the fall of our first parents; and that these Prophecies, necessarily obscure, at the time of their delivery, from the ambiguity of figurative phraseology, the extraordinary circumstances foretold, and the defects of a partial revelation, were still clear enough to keep alive the constant hope of the promised Deliverer, and precise enough, when he came at length in the fulness of time, to prove, that he really was the person promised and expected.

For this purpose it will be sufficient to select from the infinite variety of Prophetical descriptions to be found in the Old Testament, a few of the most striking, and the

the most appropriate; such as the most zealous adherents to the Mosaic Law have allowed to be descriptions of their expected Messiah, and such as the advocates of Christianity have proved, beyond all controversy, to relate exclusively to the Author and Finisher of their faith.

The scheme of Prophecy commences with the fall of man; in compassion to the afflicted sinners, God vouchsafes to tell them, " that he would put enmity between the serpent and the woman, and between his seed and her seed, and that the seed of the woman should bruise the serpent's head [g]." Taken singly, and without any connexion with the subsequent Prophecies, it would be difficult perhaps to assign a reason, why this declaration should be applied to Christ: but every Revelation that follows it is an additional assurance to us, that this is indeed the basis of them all, the first positive assurance of future Redemption.

The Jewish Church always considered it to be so; and, in later times, the Prophet

[g] Gen. iii. 15.

Isaiah

Isaiah alludes to it, as a known and established point, when he is describing the glories of Christ's kingdom, and the happiness which awaits the seed of the blessed of the Lord; for " then," says he, " dust shall be the serpent's meat [h]."

Christians at all times have agreed in considering this declaration of the Almighty to be the earliest dawn of that hope, which is now become a sure and certain confidence; " a light," as the Apostle says, " shining in a dark place, which gradually became more visible, till it opened into perfect day [i]."

After this original promise of Redemption, made by God himself, the Antediluvian world were not favoured with any farther intimation of the will of God: idolatry and irreligion were permitted to take their course, till the measure of iniquity was full: nor does it appear, that the father of the restored world, the just and righteous Noah, although gifted occasionally with some portion of the Holy Spirit,

[h] Isai. lxv. 25. [i] 2 Pet. i. 19.

for the good of his contemporaries, was empowered to make to them any more explicit declaration of the merciful intentions of Providence. The covenant which God made with him, although it is ſtyled a perpetual covenant, " the covenant of the age, or the everlaſting covenant [k];" αἰώνος δια-θήκη, as the Seventy have tranſlated it; from the time at which it was made, and the ſign or token which accompanied it, appears to have been a temporal covenant merely; a promiſe, that the earth ſhould not be deſtroyed again in the ſame way: and afterwards, when he predicts the fortunes of his ſons, the benediction of Shem, whether with our common verſions we read, " Bleſſed be the Lord God of Shem [l]," or with a great oriental critic, " Bleſſed of Jehovah, my God, be Shem [m];" this benediction cannot, I think, be underſtood to mean more than that the poſterity of Shem would be, as we know they actually were, a peculiar people, under the immediate protection and government of God.

---

[k] Gen. ix. 16.   [l] Gen. ix. 26.
[m] Kennicott's Diſſertation on the Hebrew Text, p. 561.

SERMON V.

We may go on then to the call of Abraham: at that time we learn that the extraordinary perfon, who was firft fpoken of generally as " the feed of the woman". (was defigned, that is, to be born in the flefh, and to come in the form and fubftance of a man), was to be a defcendant of the Holy Patriarch; " in thee," fays the Almighty, " fhall all families of the earth be bleffed ⁿ." Ifmael, the firft born, is afterwards excluded from the envied inheritance; he is promifed the enjoyment of temporal profperity indeed, that his dominions fhall be fertile, that he fhall be the head of a princely line, and the founder of a great and mighty nation °; but the covenant of grace meanwhile is eftablifhed with Ifaac, and in the fame manner it was afterwards taken from Efau, and limited to the pofterity of Jacob ᵖ.

To the Patriarch ᑫ Jacob it is repeated upon feveral occafions, and in various ways; by dreams and nightly vifions, and by the perfonal appearance even of the Holy One,

ⁿ Gen. xii. 3.   ° Gen. xvii. 20.
ᵖ Gen. xxvii. 29.   ᑫ Gen. xxviii. 13.

that

SERMON V.

that the blessing of Abraham was conferred upon him; and he in his last moments transfers it, in a remarkable Prophecy, to his son Judah.

" Judah," says the Patriarch, when he is announcing to his assembled sons the fortunes which are to befal them in the last days, " Judah, thou art he whom thy brethren shall praise; thy hand shall be in the neck of thine enemies, thy father's children shall bow down before thee;" " the Sceptre shall not depart from Judah, nor a lawgiver from between his feet, until Shiloh come; and unto him shall the gathering of the people be [r].

I am aware that no single Prophecy of the Old Testament has received so great a variety of interpretations, as this remarkable Prophecy of Jacob: but they are critical interpretations of words: the general meaning and intent of the Prophecy has been admitted on all hands; and whether the word Shiloh be translated, as it is in the Latin Vulgate, *Qui mittendus est*, he who

[r] Gen. xlix. 8—10.

is to be sent; whether we read with some copies of the Septuagint version, τὰ ἀποκεί-μενα αὐτῷ, the things reserved for him, or with other copies, ᾧ ἀπόκειται, he for whom it is reserved; it cannot be disputed, but that the person so alluded to is " the seed of the woman," the Messiah of the Jews, the Saviour and Redeemer of mankind.

And if we attend to the time at which the Prophecy was delivered, and the language in which it is conveyed; if we consider, that the descendants of Abraham were now recently settled in the land of Goshen; that they were to continue there in slavery for four generations; and that God thus promised them a perpetuity of temporal dominion—a continuance of it at least, until the appearance of their great Deliverer; we may conclude, that it was mercifully given to support them under the hardships which they were to endure, and to convince them, that the covenant made with their ancestors would be religiously performed.

The promise thus limited to the tribe of Judah

Judah rested there for several centuries: during the whole of the captivity in Egypt, no farther intimations are given of future redemption. But when the Jews had escaped from their long servitude, and, after all their trials and sufferings, were entering, under the guidance of their Legislator, upon the promised land, the Holy Spirit compels a Heathen Soothsayer to confirm and ratify the original covenant in the face of their enemies: " Blessed," says Balaam, in the very words which Jacob had used before him, " Blessed is he that blesseth thee, and cursed is he that curseth thee [h];" and then, in defiance of the resentment of Balak, he breaks forth into a rapturous anticipation of the triumphs of the Messiah: " I shall see him, but not now; I shall behold him, but not nigh: there shall come a star out of Jacob, and a sceptre shall rise out of Israel; out of Jacob shall come he that shall have dominion, and shall destroy him that remaineth of the city [i]."

That the Holy Spirit, when these expressions were used, might design in the

[h] Numb. xxiv. 9.   [i] Numb. xxiv. 17—19.

first

first inftance to allude to David, and his conquefts of the Moabites and the Edomites, I do not deny: but the expreffions evidently prove, that the Prophecy had a farther view to the glories and the univerfal dominion of the Meffiah.

It was now a very important crifis in the hiftory of the Jews: they were upon the point of entering that country which God had promifed to their anceftors; and at this critical period, Mofes their leader, he who had conducted them out of Egypt, who had fupported them in all their difficulties, had interceded with their God for them, and given them a civil polity, and a religion—this divine Legiflator was upon the eve of quitting them for ever. Before his departure, he comforts them with the promife of another Prophet, like unto himfelf: "The Lord thy God will raife up unto thee a Prophet, from the midft of thee, of thy brethren, like unto me; unto him fhall ye hearken [k]." If it be queftioned, whether this be a Prophecy of Chrift or not, we may appeal not only to

[k] Deut. xviii. 15.

the similitude between the blessed Jesus and the Jewish Legislator, or the degree of inspiration, or their personal conversation with the most High God, but to the undoubted authority of an inspired Apostle. St. Peter does so apply it in his first harangue to the Jews; " For Moses truly said," he argues, " unto the fathers, A Prophet shall the Lord God raise up unto you of your brethren, like unto me; him shall ye hear in all things, whatsoever he shall say unto you [x]."

Thus it was that the Jews were taught to expect in their Messiah the gifts and endowments of a Prophet; and the holy Evangelist informs us, that the multitude, when they were miraculously fed by Jesus, cried out immediately, " This is of a truth that Prophet that should come into the world [y]."

In the interval between the death of Moses and the establishment of David upon the throne of Israel, the Prophetic oracles are silent: during that period, the

[x] Acts iii. 22.   [y] John vi. 14.

chosen

chosen people were gradually extending their conquests, and acquiring a secure and permanent establishment in the land of Canaan. Then God was ever present with them, in every event of their lives; both their welfare as a community, and their happiness as individuals, were under the immediate guidance of his particular Providence. They wanted not therefore the warning voice of the Prophet, to point out to them impending dangers, or to sustain and console them under their actual pressure: the promise of Abraham, as it was now called; the covenant made by the Almighty with their righteous progenitors, in their own persons they had seen fulfilled, in one sense, by the acquisition of the conquered provinces of the Canaanites. With just confidence, therefore, they might anticipate its full and final accomplishment. But it still continued to be the general inheritance of Judah, till the establishment of David upon the throne, and then it was limited to the house and family of that prince.

"Go," says the Holy Spirit to the Prophet

phet Nathan, " Go, and tell my servant David, Thus saith the Lord—When thy days be fulfilled, and thou shalt sleep with thy fathers, I will set up thy seed after thee, which shall proceed out of thy bowels, and I will establish his kingdom. He shall build an house for my name, and I will stablish the throne of his kingdom for ever; and thine house and thy kingdom shall be established for ever before thee; thy throne shall be established for ever [z]."

If it be said, that this is a prophetical description of Solomon, and not of Christ, we may ask, whether it is true of Solomon to say, that he should be raised to the throne, when David slept with his fathers, that his kingdom should be perpetual, and his throne established for ever? It may also be asked, whether the Holy Spirit does not allude to this very Prophecy, as relating to Christ, when the Angel announces to the blessed Virgin, avowedly speaking of Christ, that the Lord should give unto him the throne of his Father David, " that he should reign over the house of Jacob for ever; and of

[z] 2 Sam. vii. 5—16.

SERMON V. 135

his kingdom there should be no end[a]?" As the temporal splendour of the Jewish nation was at its height during the reigns of David and Solomon, so also their Religion was at that time more free than ever from Pagan superstitions, and their attachment to the God of their fathers more steady and more inviolable.

But from that period, idolatrous worship began to gain ground amongst them; a succession of vicious princes corrupted the public ritual, and debased the Religion of their people. Then it was, that the Almighty thought fit to impart more liberally the gifts of his Holy Spirit, and to reveal with greater particularity, for the support, it may well be supposed, and the comfort of the righteous, who adhered to the only true God, the character and the office of him, which was to accomplish the original promise.

Whilst some of the inspired Prophets are commanded to censure the prevailing vices, and the crimes of the people; to paint in

[a] Luke i. 33.

strong colours the odious sin of Idolatry, and to call them back, if possible, to the worship of the true God; others are employed to describe, in glowing imagery, and appropriate language, the future advent of the Messiah, the glories of his kingdom, and the brilliant rewards which are reserved for the righteous. The Prophet Isaiah, being sent to announce to Ahaz the assurances of deliverance from his confederate enemies, gives him at the same time the assurance of an higher and more important deliverance, to be granted in later times. The house of David, he tells him, shall never fail, till that great deliverance takes place: and this is to happen, when " a Virgin shall conceive and bring forth a son, whose name shall be called Immanuel [b]." " There shall come forth a Rod," says the same Prophet, " out of the stem of Jesse, and a Branch shall grow out of his roots: the Spirit of the Lord shall rest upon him—with righteousness shall he judge the poor, and reprove with equity for the meek of the earth—righteousness shall be the gir-

---

[b] Isai. vii. 14.

dle

dle of his loins, and faithfulness the girdle of his reins ᶜ."

Other similar predictions of the same Prophet I pass over purposely: my wish is to trace the series of Prophetical Revelation from the beginning, not to detail all that the Prophets have spoken; otherwise it would be easy from the volume of the Evangelical Prophet, whose predictions are, in truth, a history of the Gospel—it would be easy to perceive, that Christ was to confirm the authority of his mission, and to prove his Divinity by a display of benevolent miracles; that he was to be rejected by the Jews to whom he was sent, and received by the Gentiles, although descended from the royal house of David; that his immediate Parents were to be in a state of humiliation and indigence; that he "was to be a man of sorrows, and acquainted with grief;" to be wounded for our transgressions, and to suffer for our iniquities ᵈ; and yet, that " his name should be called Wonderful, Counsellor, the mighty God, the everlasting Father, the Prince of peace ᵉ."

ᶜ Isai. xi. 1.   ᵈ Isai. liii. 3.   ᵉ Isai. ix. 6.

It would be easy to cite the passages themselves, in which those extraordinary, and to all appearance contradictory, circumstances are foretold: but I hasten to other Prophecies. About the same period of the Jewish history, the Prophet Micah marks the place in which the Messiah was to be born. " But thou, Bethlehem Ephratah," says he, " though thou be little among the thousands of Judah, yet out of thee shall he come forth unto me, that is to be Ruler in Israel; whose goings forth have been from of old, from everlasting[f]."

As we proceed in the history of the Jewish people, we find, that when the vengeance of the Almighty had overtaken them; when their city and their temple were destroyed, and their tribes led away into captivity, stronger and fuller assurances were continually given them of future deliverance.

In the days of affliction and public calamity, the unbeliever was always ready to deride the expectations of the faithful, and to accuse the Almighty of tardiness

[f] Micah v. 2.

in the execution of his promises: "Let him make speed, and hasten his work," they said, "that we may see it; and let the counsel of the Holy One of Israel draw nigh and come, that we may know[g]." God therefore vouchsafes to afford to his righteous servants, that they might refute the cavils of the gainsayers, a clearer and more explicit assurance, that his promise was never forgotten.

"Behold, the days come, saith the Lord," by the mouth of his Prophet Jeremiah, "that I will perform that good thing which I have promised unto the house of Israel, and to the house of Judah; in those days, and at that time, will I cause the Branch of Righteousness to grow up unto David; and he shall execute judgment and righteousness in the land: in those days shall Judah be saved, and Jerusalem shall dwell safely; and this is the name wherewith he shall be called, the Lord our Righteousness[h]." And when those days come, the Holy Spirit by the same Prophet declares, that the Mosaic Law shall give place to the

[g] Isai. v. 19.   [h] Jerem. xxxiii. 14.

new

new covenant. "After those days," saith the Lord, "I will put my Law in their inward parts, and write it in their hearts; and I will be their God, and they shall be my people[l]."

The Prophet Ezekiel, who was himself a captive in Chaldea, declares, that "the scattered flock shall at length be gathered into their fold; and I will set up one shepherd over them, and he shall feed them, even my servant David; he shall feed them, and he shall be their shepherd, and I the Lord will be their God, and I will make with them a covenant of peace[k]."

To the holy Daniel, when he is praying to the Almighty to take pity upon his people, and to redeem them from their captivity, the angel Gabriel announces the precise time of the Messiah's appearance upon earth. "Seventy weeks are determined upon thy people, and thy holy city, to punish their transgression, and to make an end of sins; to bring in everlasting righteousness, and to seal up the vision, and the Pro-

[l] Jerem. xxxi. 33. [k] Ezek. xxxiv. 23.

phecy,

phecy, and to anoint the moſt Holy." " Know therefore and underſtand," ſays the angel, " that from the going forth of the commandment to reſtore and to build Jeruſalem unto the Meſſiah, the prince, ſhall be ſeven weeks; and after threeſcore and two weeks ſhall Meſſiah be cut off, but not for himſelf[1]."

I forbear all comment upon this ſtriking prediction; it is impoſſible for language to be more preciſe; and it has been the ſtudy of pious and learned men, to ſhew how exactly it was verified by the event.

We are now come to the laſt period in the hiſtory of Prophecy: the Jews were to return from their captivity, and to rebuild their Temple; but it was to be far inferior to the former in external ſplendour, in decorations, and all the viſible tokens of the immediate preſence of their tutelary God.

The Holy Spirit, at this time, while it

[1] Dan. ix. 25.

ſignifies

signifies the approach of their Deliverer, uses that method of consoling the people for the evident diminution of the splendour of their Temple. "Behold," says the Prophet Zechariah, " the man whose name is the Branch; and he shall grow up out of his place, and he shall build the temple of the Lord: even he shall build the temple of the Lord; and he shall bear the glory, and shall sit and rule upon his throne, and he shall be a priest upon his throne [m]."

When the elders of Israel are looking back with regret and sorrow to what they had lost, the Holy Spirit forbids them to despair: God, by his Prophet Haggai, reminds them of the covenant he had made with their fathers, and of his fixed and inviolable purpose; and assures them, that he will make the latter house more glorious than the former. " Yet once it is a little while, and I will shake all nations, and the desire of all nations shall come; and I will fill his house with glory—the glory of this latter house shall be greater than of the former, saith the Lord of Hosts;

[m] Zechar. vi. 12.

Hosts; and in this place will I give peace[n]."

Malachi, the last of the illustrious line, assures them, at the same time, that to this their new Temple the Messiah would come. "Behold," says he, "I will send my messenger, and he shall prepare the way before me: and the Lord, whom ye seek, shall suddenly come to his temple, even the messenger of the covenant, whom ye delight in: behold, he shall come, saith the Lord of Hosts[o]."

With this express and positive assurance the vision was sealed up, and the book of Prophecy closed: for a period of more than two centuries, God left his people to reflect upon the revelations which he had already given them, to meditate continually upon the holy Oracles which were committed to their custody, and to cherish in their minds the anxious expectation of that glorious Person who was to come.

Thus I have traced, from the fall of

[n] Hagg. ii. 6.   [o] Mal. iii. 1.

man, a regular fucceffion of Prophecies, delivered at diftant intervals of time, and under very different circumftances of temporal fortune and profperity; but all combining to fhew, that at a certain time an extraordinary perfon would appear among the Jews, and all agreeing that that perfon would be of the tribe of Judah, and of the royal lineage of David; that he would be a Prophet, a King, and a Prieft; that he would come as a meffenger from God, and would proclaim a new covenant, a covenant of peace, not only to the Jews, but to the whole race of mankind.

Of the Prophecies which I have felected, almoft all relate exclufively, and in their primary fenfe, to Chrift; and for that reafon I have confined myfelf to them; not that the evidence of other Prophecies, of thofe which relate in their primary fenfe to David, or Solomon, or any other illuftrious Ifraelite, and in their fecondary only to Chrift, is not as clear, as conclufive, and as fatisfactory; for fo it certainly is: when the holy Pfalmift fays, "Thou fhalt not leave my foul in hell, neither fhalt thou

SERMON V.

thou suffer thine holy one to see corruption[p]," he is clearly speaking, not of himself, but of Christ; because, as the Apostle St. Peter argues, " David died, and was buried with his fathers, and saw corruption; Christ did not[q]; and so in every case, where a Prophecy is supposed to have a double sense, if there be any one circumstance which cannot possibly apply to the person humanly spoken of, we are to conclude, that beyond its immediate application it has a reference ultimately to Christ. The force of the Prophecy therefore is equally strong: but still, where there is any thing of ambiguity, or any thing like mystical allusion, the prediction is more exposed to cavil, and misconception, and misinterpretation; while the force of the direct Prophecies, neither the artifices of the Jewish Interpreter, nor the sneers and ridicule of the Infidel, have ever been able to weaken, or to elude.

Of the use of Prophecy in general, and of the nature of the argument with which it supplies the Christian, it is not to be expected that I should say much; it is

[p] Psalm xvi. 10.   [q] Acts ii. 27. xiii. 35.

enough

enough for my purpose to have shewn, that the Holy Spirit gradually announced with more and more perspicuity, as the fulness of time drew near, the advent of the Mediator, who was to effect the great purpose of man's redemption. Every thing beside is foreign from my subject. But as in our days the frivolous cavils and the petulant declamations of forgotten sceptics are continually received by the Sophists of the modern schools of infidelity, it would be wrong perhaps to pass over in total silence, a topic so nearly connected with the argument before us.

It was said by Porphyry, and by Celsus, in the earliest days of Christianity; it has been said by the Deists of our times; and it is one of the favourite assertions of all unbelievers, that Prophecy may be a good evidence to a Jew, or to one who believes the Divinity of the Mosaic Law, and really thinks, that the Prophetical books were dictated by God; but that it is beneath the notice of minds that are enlightened by philosophy, and which soar above the bigotry of vulgar prejudices.

What

What then if it can be proved that an event, of which at the time there was no appearance or probability whatever, was literally predicted for ages before it took place, and that it did take place at the very time and in the very manner foretold; if this can be proved, is it not to all men equally, to the Gentile as well as to the Jew, an inconteftible evidence of the interpofition of God?

If, for example, the Holy Spirit declared of Ifhmael, that "he fhould be a wild man; that his hand fhould be againft every man, and every man's hand againft him; and that his feed fhould not be numbered for multitude^r;" and we find, that this defcription is verified at this day in the numbers, the wandering life, and the unconquerable fpirit of his defcendants in Arabia: if it was faid of Canaan, that he fhould be "a fervant of fervants unto his brethren^s," and we fee his wretched pofterity ftill groaning under the yoke of the crueleft and moft oppreffive fervitude: if Tyre, Nineveh, Babylon, and Jerufalem,

^r Gen. xvi. 10—12.   ^s Gen. ix. 25.

were all destroyed precisely as the Prophet has declared that they should be, are not all these facts plain and forcible appeals to the understanding of every human being, who is capable of thinking or reasoning at all?

But the obscurity of Prophecies, it is said, gives such a latitude of interpretation, that no certain dependance is to be placed upon them. That Prophecies are obscure cannot be denied; they must all be more or less so, from the very nature of the case: for as it was not possible to reveal plainly and explicitly, during the existence of a preparatory dispensation, the great truths reserved for the latter days, it was necessary to throw over them the mysterious veil of Prophetical phraseology. But if the Prophecy be a literal one, a comparison with the event will remove the obscurity, and precisely fix its meaning; if it be figurative, the difficulty arising from figurative and symbolical expressions cannot be done away even by the event; for, as the great author of the discourse on the Use of Prophecy has observed, a figurative description

of

SERMON V.

of a future event will be figurative still, and will have all the obscurity of a figurative description as well after, as before, the event[t].

But to bring the whole question to an issue: there are in fact but two points to be considered; and no honest and impartial mind, that has satisfied itself upon those two points, can fail to look with a firm and unshaken faith, till it shall please the Almighty to make known to us, what even now continues to be shrouded from our view; for, " as yet the vision is for an appointed time[u]."

In the first place, is it possible, that the Prophecies, which so clearly and pointedly announce a Redeemer to come, should be forgeries? That they undoubtedly could not be so, must be evident to every one, who recollects, that the sacred deposit of Prophecy was committed to the care of a whole nation; that the several predictions of those inspired persons, whose cha-

[t] See Sherlock's Discourse on the Use of Prophecy.
[u] Habbak. ii. 3.

racter

racter and office the people were taught to admire and to venerate, were enrolled in the public and authentic acts of their nation; that they were recited daily in their synagogues; were guarded with the most scrupulous and jealous care; and cherished as the foundation of all their hopes, and their claims to future glory and dominion.

If under such circumstances it be impossible for an instant to entertain the suspicion of a forgery, or to question the authenticity of the Prophetical descriptions of our blessed Lord; the next point to be ascertained is, whether the person so described did actually appear in the world: did he come at the time previously specified? Was he really the descendant of David? And did he claim to be the messenger of God, and the founder of a new covenant? "Did he raise and support the poor and lowly in spirit?" Was he " eyes to the blind, and feet to the lame?" And did the blessing of them that were ready to perish come upon him? Did he, lastly, assert, that he was come to redeem mankind? Did he
" die

"die for our sins, and rise again for our justification?" If all this be true, if it be an undoubted historical fact, that a person, with such claims, and such pretensions, did actually appear in Judea, the conclusion is immediate: we have only to acknowledge, as Philip did to Nathaniel, that "we have found him of whom Moses in the Law, and all the Prophets, did write, Jesus of Nazareth, the son of Joseph [x]."

[x] John i. 45.

SERMON VI.

JEREMIAH xlvi. 28.

FEAR THOU NOT, O JACOB MY SERVANT, SAITH THE LORD: FOR I AM WITH THEE; FOR I WILL MAKE A FULL END OF ALL THE NATIONS WHITHER I HAVE DRIVEN THEE: BUT I WILL NOT MAKE A FULL END OF THEE.

HAVING shewn in my former Lectures what were the great uses of the preparatory dispensations of Judaism, it is now time for me to consider the admirable methods of God's providence, by which it was contrived, that the fortunes of the Jewish people, their political revolutions,

tions, and their alternate changes from power and prosperity to humiliation and slavery, should all contribute to promote the great purpose of preserving in the world the knowledge of the true God, and of preparing the way for the promised Messiah.

It is reasonable to expect, that a nation set apart and distinguished from all others, in the essential features of laws, customs, and religion, should also be distinguished by some striking peculiarity in their external circumstances, that the vicissitudes of their fortunes would be more uncommon, and that their happiness and their misery would carry with them some indications of the design, for which they were originally separated from the rest of mankind.

In the declaration, by which the Prophet is ordered to console the companions of his captivity, a difference is marked between the conduct of the Almighty to his chosen people, and to the rest of mankind: " Fear not, O Jacob," saith the Lord; " other nations I will utterly destroy—
thine

SERMON VI. 155

thine enemies, thofe who have been the minifters of my vengeance to punifh thee, fhall be fwept away from the face of the earth: but of thee I will not make a full end."

This then is the peculiarity by which the Jews, as a nation, were ftrongly contrafted, in their external circumftances, with every other nation exifting; that they were not at all affected by thofe circumftances of alliance, of commerce, of migration, or of conqueft, which either infenfibly change the manners and habits of a people, or force them reluctantly into new affociations, till every trace of their original character be loft: that although unfortunate as no people ever were (for they ftrictly verified what their Legiflator had foretold, " that no mifery fhould be like their mifery"), they tenacioufly preferved the remembrance of the promife of Abraham: although fcattered and difperfed over the face of the globe, their national character was as diftinct as if they had never quitted the confines of the promifed land: and although reduced by the ravages of inceffant wars,

and

and the severe hardships of servitude, their population continually increased; and the remnant, to whose sorrow and contrition God once more granted the possessions of their forefathers, became again in no long time a flourishing and powerful people.

Thus it was contrived by the wisdom of God, for the instruction and benefit of all his creatures, that the whole **tenor of the** Jewish history should contain a constant display of his particular providence; and as it hath pleased him, that the events of that history should be recorded for our use, under the immediate guidance of his Holy Spirit, we are to profit from the lessons it conveys, as much as those who were spectators of the fact recorded: nor are we left to the fallible and uncertain conclusions of our own reason; for this history (it is the observation of a great man, and I will give it in his own expressive language) hath herein a singular prerogative above all that have been written by the most sufficient of merely **human authors**—it setteth down expresly the **true and first causes of** all that happened, not imputing " the death of

SERMON VI.

of Ahab to his over forwardness in battle," the " ruin of his family to the security of Jehoram in Jezreel ;" nor the " victories of Hazael to the great commotions raised in Israel, by the coming of Jehu; but referring all unto the will of God, I mean, unto his revealed will [a]."

It is not that the fates and fortunes of the rest of mankind were not as much under the control and direction of God's providence, as those of the people of Israel: but the interposition of that providence was not so visible, nor so evident to man.— In the annals of prophane history, we pass to the first great Origin of all, through the medium of secondary causes ; and too often, it is to be feared, the mind stops there, and is content to attribute the effect produced to the immediate cause before us; to the operation of the passions, or the appetites, or the understanding of man, without raising its thoughts to him who uses the agency of human affections, and human appetites, to bring to pass the purposes of his

[a] Ralegh's History of the World, Book II. Part I. chap. xxi.

own eternal will. But when we open the sacred Volume of inspiration, the case is widely different; the transition from the effect to the first cause is immediate; the will of God is announced, and the event follows that will, without any delay, or any chain of intermediate operations—success and misfortune, defeat and victory—regularly follow the performance or the violation of the original compact made between God and his people. Thus we are brought, as it were, into the very counsels of the Almighty; and the revealed will of God being our guide, we can be at no loss to combine the principal events, to bring them together under one view, and to trace them ultimately to that one great design, which connects and harmonizes the whole.

God, when he first summoned the father of the Jewish people from his native country, expressly told him, that his descendants should become a numerous people, numerous as " the sand of the sea, or the dust of the earth [b]." The holy Jacob is told, " that he should spread to the East and the West,

[b] Gen. xii. 2. xiii. 16.

the

the North and the South[c]." But when the Patriarchal family went down to Egypt with their flocks, what reason had they to expect the accomplishment of this promise? They were few in number, and poor and inefficient in their circumstances. In the common course of things, even if they had been favoured and cherished throughout by the Princes of Egypt, as they were at first; if their lives had been tranquil and easy, and their resources affluent, ages and generations must have passed away, before they could have been numerous enough to justify in any degree the expectations, which the promise made to their ancestors had raised. But we know that their lives were neither easy nor undisturbed; a spirit of jealousy, which the rapidity of their increase seems first to have excited, induced the Egyptians to harrass and oppress these new settlers, in whom they expected to find a rival, and an enemy, and perhaps a conqueror. Laborious tasks were imposed upon them, under which it was conceived their strength must fail; the rigour of their servitude was increased, and every scheme,

[c] Gen. xxviii. 14.

that the bitterest malice could devise, was executed, in order to check and depress them; but in vain: for, as their own historian informs us, " the more they were afflicted the more they multiplied and grew[d]." And when the days of their bondage were accomplished, they came forth, in defiance of all the attempts to detain them in slavery, or to reduce them to insignificance, a numerous and wealthy people.

It was this miraculous increase, under circumstances so inauspicious, that they were afterwards commanded by their Legislator to commemorate, when they offered up to God the first-fruits of their harvest. The form of thanksgiving, which the Law prescribed upon that solemn occasion, commences with a comparison between their first entry into Egypt, when they were going to select food for their support, and their triumphal departure from it, with the mighty sign and wonder accompanying their progress: the Angel of God continually watching over them, and the Almighty arm uplifted, to check and discom-

[d] Exod. i. 12.

fit

fit the hoſt of their purſuers: "thou ſhalt ſpeak and ſay," ſaid the Law, "before the Lord thy God, A Syrian ready to periſh was my father; and he went down into Egypt and ſojourned there with a few, and became there a nation great, mighty, and populous[e]."

This was the firſt ſtep in the gradual accompliſhment of the temporal covenant: redeemed from oppreſſion and from ſlavery, enriched with the treaſures of their enemies, and evidently protected and guarded by God, the people of Iſrael now anticipated with confidence the poſſeſſion of that good land which had been promiſed to their fathers: but they were not aware of the trials and the difficulties which ſtill awaited them; that they were to wander for forty years, without any fixed or regular ſettlement, in the pathleſs deſert before them; and that the land of plenty was only to be acquired by the conqueſt of the warlike nations who then poſſeſſed it. On the events which befel them in the wilderneſs it would be idle to

[e] Deut. xxvi. 5.

dwell;

dwell; it is known to every one, that as the course, which they took, deviated in many instances from that which human prudence, or human foresight, would have chosen; so the mode of their subsistence, their dress, and their diet, during their tedious marches, were all miracles, and only to be accounted for by the constant interference of God. So their own great leader told them; " I have led you forty years," said he, " in the wilderness: your cloaths are not waxen old upon you, and thy shoe is not waxen old upon thy foot: ye have not eaten bread, neither have ye drunk wine or strong drink, that ye might know, that I am the Lord your God[f]." The great object then of this sojourning in the desert, and this continual display of miracles, was to impress upon their minds a thorough conviction of the power of God, and an implicit faith in his promises. Let us suppose then, that all these trials are past, that they are now a distinct nation, with a code of judicial ordinances, a system of morality, and a ritual of worship, all vouchsafed to them by God himself; that

[f] Deut. xxix. 5.

Moses,

Moses, their Deliverer, their Mediator, and their Guide, after a formal ratification of the covenant with the Almighty, and a prophetic delineation of the blessings and the curses which would inevitably attend their obedience, or disobedience, has departed from them for ever; that, under the auspices of his successor Joshua, the tribes are settled in their respective allotments, precisely as the holy Patriarch Jacob, in his parting benediction[g], and Moses after him[h], had predicted that they would be settled.

It is scarcely credible how short an interval had passed, before this perverse and ungrateful people not only forgot all that they had been taught, and all that they had suffered, but violated even the express condition upon which they knew that their existence as a nation depended. Instead of acting as the delegates of God, and the ministers of his vengeance, to punish the idolatrous Canaanites to the uttermost, they became their partners and companions in wickedness, and offered up at

[g] Gen. xlix.   [h] Deut. xxxiii.

the shrines of the Syrian Deities of Baal and Ashtaroth, those acts of praise and adoration which they knew to belong exclusively to the one true God: thus, although God, as it is said, had " rolled away from them the reproach of Egypt[1]," a greater reproach, and the stain of fouler impiety, was fixed upon them.

During the administration of their judges, the Jewish history presents to us little more than a picture of their strange infatuation and blindness, and of the mercy and long suffering of God; a constant repetition of the same crimes, and the same punishments, the same repentance, and the same rewards: idolatry punished by slavery, and sincere acknowledgement of the offence, and return to the worship of the true God, rewarded by a restoration to liberty, and the possession of their promised inheritance. Of this dispensation of providence, we cannot fail to remark, that the mode of punishment, and the mode of reward, which God thought fit to adopt, were calculated in an eminent degree, not only to correct the idolatrous

pro-

SERMON VI.

propensities of the Israelites, but to imprefs surrounding nations with a belief of the one true God, and thus to extend more widely the foundations of true religion.

These nations—the nations, that is, who from antient times had posseffed the promifed land, and the countries bordering upon it, were either the descendants of Canaan, or, more properly speaking, of Ham, or the relations and posterity of Abraham, who gradually migrated to the territories originally designed for them by the Almighty: of Lot, for instance, came the two great families of Moab and Ammon; of Esau, the Idumæans; of Madian, the Madianites; and of Ismael, the Ismaelites and the Amalekites: and to the hatred which the Canaanites naturally would feel for an invader, who was come to rob them of all their poffeffions, to break down their images and their altars, to destroy their hallowed groves, and to deface every vestige of the religion of their ancestors, the children of the Patriarch Abraham added the animofity of rivals; of rivals contending for that glorious inheritance, which had

had been promised originally to all the seed of Abraham, without any distinction or limitation. In the sight of these nations, therefore, no punishment and no reward could be so impressive, or so awful, as the grant or the deprivation of that country, in which they all supposed they had a right to participate. This therefore was the scene which the Almighty chose for a display of his power; from thence he drove his people when they forgot him, or rebelled against him, and forced them to bend their neck under the yoke of the very rivals who hated and despised them; and thither he brought them back again, when they were repentant and sorrowful, with " a mighty hand, and outstretched arm," by the single and unassisted efforts of his chosen servants, of Sampson, of Gideon, of Jepthah, and Deborah. Thus it was, that, during the alternate vicissitudes of comfort and slavery, the nation still continued to increase in numbers and in power; and if we go on to the times of their monarchy, when the servant of God was called from the sheep-fold to sit upon the throne of Israel, when " the fame of him

him went out unto all lands, and the fear of him through all nations;" we find, that in repeated conflicts they have constantly been victorious, that they have gradually triumphed over their enemies, and extended their dominions almost, although not entirely, to the boundaries which God had fixed himself, from the "Red Sea even unto the sea of the Philistine, and from the desert unto the river[k]."

To the extent of country which David acquired by conquest, under the peaceful sway of his successor, they added the advantages of commerce. His alliance with Hiram of Tyre, and his marriage with the Egyptian Princess, contributed to aid and promote the plans which his own wisdom had devised; and from the ports of Elath and Eziongeber, which he improved and fortified, the wealth of Africa and India flowed into Jerusalem, until, as the sacred Historian informs us, " cedars[l] were as sycamore trees that are in the vale for abundance, and silver in Jerusalem as stones." If, from this period of splendour

[k] Exod. xxiii. 31.   [l] 1 Kings x. 27.

and prosperity, we go on to the revolt of the ten tribes, and the separation of the two kingdoms of Israel and Judah, it appears, that the ancient fondness for idolatrous devotion, which had long lain dormant, revived with increased ardor. The worship of the golden calves at Bethel justified the practice, and led the way to all the monstrous corruptions, and the prophane rites, which the kings of Israel were eager to sanction and encourage. In vain did God by the mouth of his holy Prophets warn them of their danger, and command them to return to the way of righteousness which they had forsaken; neither the picture of ruin and desolation, which the Holy Spirit was continually presenting to their imaginations, nor the partial evils which they suffered, nor the removal of the flower of their countrymen into Egypt and Chaldea, had any effect upon this deluded people: they persevered in the open abuse of their law, and the contempt and defiance of God, until their city and their temple were destroyed, and the whole nation reduced to slavery. During the whole period of this their greatest and

and longest captivity, the providence of God was watching over them continually: they were kept distinct in every respect, and separate from their conquerors. Of Jehoiakim their King, it is said, that " his throne was set above the throne of the Kings that were in Babylon ᵐ." Many of the principal leaders were raised to situations of power and confidence; and the great body of the people were ordered, by a public decree, to take wives for them and for their sons, that they " might be increased there," as the Prophet tells us, " and not diminished ⁿ."

Repentance and a confession of their guilt, after the period had elapsed, which was ordained before of God, produced their customary effect; and the people were restored to their country; but not the whole people.

Of the twelve tribes, two only, those of Judah and Benjamin, with the Levites, were permitted to return to Judea. From that time to the present, the fate of the

ᵐ 2 Kings xxv. 28.   ⁿ Jer. xxix. 6.

other

other ten tribes has continued to be involved in obscurity. Where they have subsisted, what their situation has been, and whether at this day traces of them are to be found, as modern travellers inform us, in the plains of Hindostan and China, are questions of curiosity, which have no concern with our subject: and whatever their fate may have been, the prediction of the Prophet would equally have been verified, that " within threescore and five years, Ephraim shall be broken, that it be not a people °." Judah meanwhile, to whom belonged the adoption and the glory ᵖ; and of whom, " as in the flesh, Christ was to come ;" he of whom his Father, in his last prophetic benediction, had said, " that he should be more numerous and more powerful than his brethren ᑫ; and that his polity, as a nation, should not be dissolved, till the actual appearance of the great Redeemer ;" Judah did return to the inheritance of his ancestors, and rebuilt the holy Temple of God.

From the period of their restoration, the

° Isai. vii. 8. ᵖ Rom. ix. 4. ᑫ Gen. xlix.

Jews

SERMON VI.

Jews seem entirely to have conquered that fatal attachment to the idolatry of their Heathen neighbours, which had already involved them in so many calamities. And as if the warning of Malachi, who closed the illustrious line of inspired Prophets, was perpetually sounding in their ears, " remember ye the law of Moses, my servant, which I commanded unto him in Horeb, for all Israel [r]," their observance of the Mosaic Law, of its precepts, and its ordinances, appears to have been more scrupulous, and more exact, than it had been at any former period of their history.

In the mean time, their political situation was more secure, and more settled: the Princes of Persia, whose vast empire extended over the greater part of the Eastern hemisphere, from India, as it is said in the holy Scriptures of the kingdom of Ahasuerus, from India even unto Ethiopia, over one hundred and seven and twenty provinces [s]"—these powerful Princes be-

---

[r] Mal. iv. 4.   [s] Esth. i. 1.

stowed

stowed upon the Jewish nation peculiar marks of their favour; and in later times, the great conqueror of the world, who broke this mighty empire, and divided its provinces amongst his followers, in the career of his victories spared the holy city, and granted to its inhabitants all the privileges, and all the immunities, which their ancestors had enjoyed.

If at this period we look to the circumstances of the Jews in their own country, we find that they were secure from the attack of surrounding nations, which before were harassing them with perpetual incursions. Moab was gone: the Holy Spirit had declared, that it would be so, that " the spoiler should come upon every city, and no city should escape: that the valley also should perish, and the plain be destroyed¹." And this had been actually accomplished: the Philistines also, and the Ammonites, had yielded to their fate. And Esau was actually in servitude under the Jews: the very people whom they

¹ Jer. xlviii. 8.

had

had scorned and hated, as the possessors of the birth-right of their anceſtors.

If we look abroad to diſtant countries, and to cities far removed from Jeruſalem, we ſee the followers of Moſes received every where with peculiar marks of favour and diſtinction. At Athens, Corinth, and Epheſus, and all the principal cities of Greece, they had their own ſynagogues; in Egypt, they had their Temple, their Magiſtrates, and a Government of their own: at Antioch, the Law of Moſes was preached continually, and even in Rome: jealous as the Romans were of any privileges, and much as they diſliked the Jewiſh people, there were times, when the Jews were permitted to legiſlate for themſelves.

In the conflicts between the Macedonian Princes of Syria and Egypt, Judea, from its ſituation, was naturally expoſed to perpetual incurſions: but of theſe Princes almoſt all but one were the friends and protectors of the Jewiſh nation. That one indeed, as their Prophets had foretold, was a cruel and mercileſs perſecutor: he defaced

the

the holy city, plundered the temple, and pillaged and deſtroyed the inhabitants. But the vengeance of God overtook him, and in his laſt moments he avows what he believes to be the cauſe of his ſufferings: " The ſleep," ſays he, " is gone from mine eyes, and my heart faileth for very care : and I thought with myſelf, into what tribulation am I come, and how great a flood of miſery it is wherein I now am! for I was bountiful and beloved in my power. But now I remember the evils that I did at Jeruſalem; that I took all the veſſels of gold and ſilver that were therein, and ſent to deſtroy the inhabitants of Judea without a cauſe. I perceive therefore, that for this cauſe theſe troubles are come upon me; and behold I periſh through great grief, in a ſtrange land ᵘ." Such was the confeſſion of Antiochus; and while he was execrated for his cruelty, the nation, which he had oppreſſed, was admired for the intrepidity of its leaders, its undaunted fortitude, and its zeal in the defence of its religion.

It happened however, that unfortunately

ᵘ Macc. vi. 10. Polyb. Fragm. p. 997. edit. Caſaub.

their own internal divisions soon opened the way for a new conqueror; and the Jewish nation became at length the tributaries of Rome: but still they continued a distinct people; and with the legions of Rome in their city, the religion of Moses was the same, and the authority of the Sanhedrim continued inviolate.

In this latter æra of their history, therefore, it appears, that they were exposed to fewer vicissitudes, and fewer calamities, than in earlier times; that as they had not been contaminated by the vices and the crimes of their forefathers, so they had escaped their awful punishments: they had not been driven from their country, under the scourge of the oppressor, into exile and captivity; but, with few exceptions, had been permitted to cultivate in peace the inheritance of their forefathers. And in this state they continued, until the appointed time arrived, the time which had been determined from old, upon them and upon the holy city, and until the measure of their iniquity was full.

If we look back to the principal epochs

in their history, to their deliverance from Egypt, their settlement in Canaan, the flourishing days of their monarchy, their captivity in Babylon, and their subsequent establishment in Judea; it is evident beyond all doubt, that they were miraculously preserved from that ruin, in which it is the fate of all nations to be involved, either by the violence of conquest, or the silent and imperceptible attacks of time: that God always remembered the covenant which he had made with their fathers, the covenant of Abraham, Isaac, and Jacob; and that, when in the latter days the Messiah came unto his own, he found them still existing, with a civil polity, and a Religion distinct from that of any other nation in the world.

But more than this; if we look to them under all their circumstances, and all their revolutions of fortune, whether they were prosperous or unfortunate, whether they were at rest within the fertile borders of Palestine, " every man under his vine, and under his fig-tree [x]," or " mourning in slavery by the waters of Babylon [y];" we

---

[x] Mic. iv. 4.   [y] Psalm cxxxvii. 1.

SERMON VI.

fee them ftill as the agents of the providence of God, who by thefe means was fecretly carrying on his great defign, and preparing the world for the introduction of the Gofpel.

It is impoffible to fuppofe upon any principles of human reafon, that their earlieft captivity in Egypt, and their extraordinary deliverance, had not a powerful effect upon the minds of all who witneffed, and all who heard of it; the miracles of Mofes, the rapid augmentation of the Ifraelites, and the deftruction of the mighty hoft of Pharoah, were all convincing evidences, that this fingular people were under the guidance and protection of a God, far fuperior in power to the fabled divinities of Egypt.

It is equally impoffible to fuppofe, that the conqueft of Canaan, with all the circumftances attending it, the defeat of numerous armies by fmall bodies of men, and fometimes even by individuals, the immediate overthrow of fortified cities, without any of the ordinary operations of war; and, above all, the exact conformity of the fucceffes or

N   the

the failures of the Jews, to the observance or neglect of their religion—it is not possible to suppose, that they who were witnesses of facts so unusual, and so contrary to the common course of human events, would not frequently be induced to turn from the lying vanities of Paganism, to the worship of the living God. The sacred Historians inform us, that this was the case, that the number of proselytes increased continually, and that in the beginning of the reign of Solomon they were found to be " an hundred and fifty thousand, and three thousand and six hundred [z]." The Jewish commentators assert, with what foundation I cannot pretend to determine, that, in the days of David and Solomon, the Sanhedrim were very cautious in their admission of the numerous Gentile converts to the privileges of Judaism, lest fear of David's power, and admiration of the glory and splendour of Solomon, should have been their sole motives for wishing to join in the worship of the Israelites. If this be true, we must suppose, that the number of converts in those days was very considerable; and this number

[z] 2 Chron. ii. 17.

was

was certainly increased during the captivity of the Jews in Babylon.

During the whole of that period, the Prophets of the captivity were continually denouncing the wrath of God against Idolators, and authenticating the reality of their inspiration, by the evidence of miracles—and not only the inspired Prophets, but all the devout Israelites, all the sincere believers in the God of their fathers, were constantly exhorting their conquerors to believe and be converted; "Confess him," is the language of a pious captive to his countrymen, "Confess him before the Gentiles, ye children of Israel, for he hath scattered us among them: there declare his greatness, and extol him before all the living, for he is our Lord; and he is the God of our fathers: in the land of my captivity will I praise him, and declare his might and majesty to a sinful nation [a]."

From the time that the captives in Babylon were restored by Cyrus, they who were left behind seem gradually to have

---

[a] Tob. xii. 3, 4.

dispersed themselves into different settlements. The communication between distant nations was becoming every day more easy and more frequent. The Asiatic invasions of Greece had shewn the possibility of an intercourse between the two continents; and the Macedonian conquest of Asia effected this intercourse. Thus the knowledge of the true God, of the Laws, and the Religion, which he had himself presented to his chosen people, was communicated to every part of the civilized world; and in the days of the Apostles, "there were dwelling at Jerusalem Jews, devout men, from every nation under heaven [b]." In the mean time, that the great end of this dispersion might be fulfilled; that the knowledge of the one true God, and of his gracious intentions to mankind, might be diffused more generally, and with greater facility; it was ordained, that the sacred Oracles of his word should be promulgated in that language, which was not only the language of philosophy and literature, but the medium of general communication to the Gentile world. When the Greek ver-

[b] Acts ii. 5.

sion

sion of the holy Scriptures was made by the Jews of Alexandria, it was in the power of every Gentile to study the history of Religion; to trace the origin of mankind; their fall from innocence; the promise of redemption; and the prophetic delineations of that glorious person, by whom it was to be effected.

It cannot therefore be doubted, that whether the Almighty scattered his peculiar people over the face of the earth, or whether he preserved a remnant in Jerusalem, it was equally his intention, by both these acts of his providence, ultimately to promote the one great design of introducing the Christian faith.

I cannot however close the subject without observing, that the prophecy, from which I have taken the words of my text, points to a farther accomplishment.

The proud oppressors of God's peculiar people have long ago been humbled to the dust: of them God has made a full end: their power, their wealth, and their magnificence,

nificence, are gone for ever. If we afk for Egypt, who was once the glory of the world, the parent of arts and fciences, and the great mart of induftry and commerce, has fhe not long ago exactly verified the declarations of the Prophet, that " fhe fhould become a bafe kingdom [c]; that there fhould be no more a prince of the land of Egypt [d]; and that Ham in his pofterity fhould be a fervant of fervants [e]?" If for Babylon, is fhe not become " a defolation, a dry land, and a wildernefs; a land wherein no man dwelleth, neither doth any fon of man pafs thereby [f]?" If for Nineveh, did not God long ago accomplifh what he had faid, that " the gate of the rivers fhould be opened, and the palaces diffolved [g];" and that " with an overrunning flood, he would make an utter end of the place thereof [h]?" Thus the Almighty hath made an end of the nations, who were the enemies and the oppreffors of his people: but of them he hath not made an end. He hath driven them, it is true, from the holy city, and given up the land of pro-

[c] Ezek. xxix. 14.   [d] Ezek. xxx. 13.   [e] Gen. ix. 25.
[f] Jer. li. 43.   [g] Nah. ii. 6.   [h] Nah. i. 8.

mife

mife to be trod under foot by the Heathen.

But of the people he hath not made a full end: though perfecuted, oppreffed, and harraffed, as they have been, with a cruelty, of which it is difficult to conceive the exiftence in any civilized country, and ftill more in any Chriftian country, their numbers have always increafed, they continue " to grow and multiply," and they are at this day to be found in every nation under heaven.

Why they are thus referved, or what ends of Divine providence they are to accomplifh, we cannot pronounce with certainty, until it fhall pleafe the Almighty to remove the veil from our eyes: and that will not be, till all human diftinctions of religion fhall be done away; till the Jew, the Gentile, and the Mahometan, fhall unite in a common faith, and we fhall all " be one fold under one Shepherd, Jefus Chrift the Righteous [i]."

[i] John x. 16.   Ezek. xxxvii. 22.

SERMON VII.

DANIEL ii. 20, 21, 22.

BLESSED BE THE NAME OF GOD FOR EVER AND EVER; FOR WISDOM AND MIGHT ARE HIS: AND HE CHANGETH THE TIMES AND THE SEASONS; HE REMOVETH KINGS, AND SETTETH UP KINGS; HE GIVETH WISDOM UNTO THE WISE, AND KNOWLEDGE TO THEM THAT KNOW UNDERSTANDING; HE REVEALETH THE DEEP AND SECRET THINGS; HE KNOWETH WHAT IS IN THE DARKNESS, AND THE LIGHT DWELLETH WITH HIM.

IN this simple and sublime strain of devotion, the holy Prophet offers up his thanksgiving to God, for that communication of the Divine Spirit, which had recently

cently been vouchsafed to the prayers of himself and his companions. To this man of the captives of Judah, as he was invidiously styled by the attendants of Nebuchadnezzar, God had given that insight into futurity, which was denied to the magicians and astrologers of Babylon; and he was commanded, by the great revealer of all secrets, to unfold to the anxious Monarch the revolutions of earthly governments in regular succession, until the establishment of that glorious kingdom, before which all human dominions, all principalities, and all powers, were to fade away, and sink into obscurity.

In that vision which the holy Daniel was impowered by God to interpret, that vision which had troubled the spirit of Nebuchadnezzar, had broken his rest, and given him up a prey to sorrow and inquietude; under the symbol of an image composed of different materials, the Holy Spirit had represented the four great Monarchies, which were successively to rule the civilized world.

After

SERMON VII.

After an interval of several years, the vision was repeated, under different symbols, to the Prophet himself, and the Angel of God was the interpreter. The four Beasts, like the component parts of the great image, were explained to be the powerful Monarchies, which were to succeed each other in a regular order: the fourth to be different from the other three, " dreadful, and terrible, and strong exceedingly [a];" to devour the whole earth, and to tread it down, and break it in pieces.

Of both these visions it may be observed, that the prophetical history does not terminate with the dissolution and dismemberment of the fourth Monarchy, but extends its view through a long succession of ages, to the triumphant dominion of the Son of Man; the everlasting kingdom, which all dominions were to serve and obey; and thus it connects under one view the establishment of Christianity, and the fates of the Christian Church, with the various revolutions in the political situation of mankind. It would be foreign to my purpose

[a] Dan. vii. 7.

to enter into a minute examination of these awful revelations. I follow the general sense of the most approved commentators, in supposing the four kingdoms of the Prophet to be those of Assyria, Persia, Macedon, and Rome. I have referred to the prophecy itself only for the purpose of shewing, that while the chosen race of Abraham were fulfilling the purposes for which they were separated, and distinguished as a peculiar people, the Almighty Disposer of all events was gradually bringing the rest of mankind into that state, which he judged to be the most proper, for receiving and propagating the Gospel of righteousness.

When we turn from the sacred records of inspiration to the annals of prophane history, with the same design of tracing the gradual preparations for the introduction of the Christian religion, there is a wide difference in the degree of certainty, which attends our conclusions. I had occasion before to mark this difference, and to observe, that, in the one case, the interposition of Providence is immediate, and evident at once; the agent of God is expressly commanded

manded to execute the counsels of Almighty wisdom; and whether he be the appointed minister of vengeance, or of grace, we not only see that he is appointed to dispense the blessing, or to inflict the punishment, as the people are obedient or rebellious, but we are also told distinctly why he is so appointed; and thus the effect produced can always be assigned, not to the agency of man, but to its true and original cause, the will of God. This could not be the case, where the will of man was permitted to act entirely for itself, without the continual interference and control of God's particular providence; and in this consisted the striking contrast between the relative situation of the Jew and the Gentile: the Jew was subject to the particular authority of God as his sovereign; the Gentile was under the protection of his general providence, and amenable to his general laws, as the moral Governor of the world: so that, whilst every act of the Jew, whether individually considered or collectively as a state, was immediately marked by the sanction or the disapprobation of God, as their supreme Governor,

vernor, the Gentile was permitted to follow, without interruption, the bias originally given to his nature; his paffions, his affections, his appetites, all tending ultimately to produce the good defigned by God, while the wifdom which planned the important end, and the power which directed to that one end all the varied combinations of human conduct, was far removed from mortal eyes.

On this account it naturally becomes a tafk of greater difficulty, to reafon upon the caufes of all the complicated events in the hiftory of the Gentile world: there is more danger of deviating from the truth into unprofitable conjectures, and more neceffity therefore for that diftruft of our own opinions, which ought ever to guide our enquiries into the hidden and myfterious ways of Providence. Surely it is reafonable to prefume, that the Almighty Governor of the world in his good time would bring his creatures into that particular ftate of fociety, and of government, which was likely to be moft favourable to the eftablifhment of the religion, which

in

in his mercy he intended to reveal to them; and what that ftate would be, muft be collected from the character of the religion, and the mode in which it was to be propagated.

Chriftianity was not to be like the religions of Paganifm, a partial fyftem of worfhip, confined to the country in which it was firft taught, or to the people who firft embraced it; it was defigned to be the religion of the world, and in God's good time the glad tidings of falvation were to be communicated to " all languages, people, and nations, under heaven." But in what way was this to be effected? and were the glorious doctrines of man's redemption from fin, and reftoration to eternal life, to be generally diffufed over the civilized world? and by what force, or what artifice, was that fabric of error and falfehood, which the fuperftition of the Gentiles had reared with all its fplendid accompaniments of facrifices, and feftivals, and oracles, to be demolifhed for ever?

The Providence of God defigned from the

the very beginning, that this great change in the religious state of mankind should be produced by methods which human prudence never would have devised, and by instruments which the vanity of human reason would have rejected, had they been proposed, as totally inadequate to such a task. It was not his intention to overpower the feeble minds of his creatures by a display of pomp and majesty, nor to fascinate their senses by the allurements of art and elegance, nor to force their will, by the sword of the conqueror, reluctantly to accept the proffered terms of salvation. The pure wisdom of heaven was to be taught by a few unlearned men, selected from the lower classes of society, and the most ordinary occupations of civil life: they were to go forth alone, and unprotected, and without any even of the customary provisions for distant expeditions: they were to traverse remote countries, and to preach the cross of Christ; sometimes to a refined and polished audience at Corinth, at Athens, or at Rome; and sometimes to a horde of uncivilized Barbarians in Iberia, or Gaul, or Britain.

It

SERMON VII.

It is clear therefore, that this gracious defign of diffufing the light of the Gofpel of truth over thofe diftant nations who " were fitting in darknefs and the fhadow of death," could never be fo well effected, as when countries the moft removed from each other in natural pofition were connected by a bond of union under one common government, when habitual intercourfe had been eftablifhed between them, and it was eafy to pafs from one to the other, without danger or interruption.

It was to this point, that the Providence of God gradually directed all the great revolutions in the political ftate of mankind : and whoever meditates upon the inftructive page of hiftory, with this idea in his mind, cannot fail to obferve, in how many inftances the plans, which were formed by legiflators and philofophers, to connect and affociate diftant countries with each other, and the fchemes of aggrandizement and univerfal dominion, which were the delight of ambitious conquerors, were all unexpectedly fruftrated, when upon the principles of human policy fuccefs appeared to
be

be certain, until the proper time arrived, ὁ ἴδιος καιρὸς, as the Apostle calls it, the time which Almighty wisdom had chosen before the world began, as the properest and the best, for the actual appearance of the Messiah upon earth.

It would not be possible for me, in the compass of a single lecture, to enter into the detail of facts which involve the history of mankind, from the earliest ages to the æra of Christianity, or to mark all the circumstances in the succession of the four monarchies, which bear in legible characters the impression of the finger of God. It is enough for my purpose to shew, that at a certain period of time fore-ordained of God, and not before, the civilized world was to be placed under the dominion of one particular people, and that with a view to facilitate the propagation of the Christian religion : and I do it in the hope, that many of my hearers, whose early youth is directed in this place to the study of prophane history, will learn to consider that history, not merely as a jejune narrative of uninteresting facts, nor as a splendid argu-

argument for the pen of the hiftorian, or the orator, but as a record of the power and providence of God; that they may accuftom their minds to look beyond fecondary caufes; and inftead of attributing, with mere worldly men, the rife and growth of empires to the valour of the conqueror, and the fagacity of the lawgiver, and their decay and fubverfion to the machinations of the factious, or the attacks of foreign enemies; that they may refer all to the over-ruling providence of God, of him " to whom belongeth the power and the might, who changeth the times and the feafons, who fetteth up and removeth kings."

It feems ever to have been the courfe of human affairs, that a fmall community fhould rife from very poor and low beginnings, till in procefs of time it became a flourifhing and mighty empire. The virtues neceffary to an infant ftate, fimplicity, frugality, temperance, patience, and valour, while they formed the character of its citizens, enabled them at the fame time gradually to extend the limits of their poffeffions: firft the conqueft of their immediate

diate neighbours, then of remote countries, by degrees give it opulence and power, till in time power and opulence introduce thofe vices which inevitably terminate in the decay and corruption of every political body. Thus it has often happened, that a mighty empire has fallen in a moment, even in the height of its profperity, and when, to the narrow views of human policy, its permanence and ftability appeared to be moft certain; " dies, hora, momentum fufficit evertendis dominationibus quæ adamantinis credebantur radicibus effe fundatæ [b]."

By this courfe of events, the moral government of God has ever been vindicated, becaufe the misguided appetites and paffions of human nature thus eventually bring upon themfelves their own punifhment: and, in the mean time, the viciffitudes of profperity and misfortune; the alternate elevation and depreffion, which the various nations of the world experienced; and the changes from abfolute dominion to ruin and to fervitude, tended ultimately to produce that general fubjection to one

[b] Vide Cafaub. Præfat. quæ Polybii Hifter. præmittitur.

power,

power, which was neceffary to the purpofes of God.

If we carry back our refearches to the earlieft age of mankind, after the confufion of languages, and the difperfion of thofe tribes who had attempted to form a fettlement in the plains of Shina, the hiftory of every nation, but that of the chofen people and their immediate neighbours, contains little more than fabulous accounts of migrations and early fettlements, with doubtful claims to preeminence, and to antiquity. The firft powerful monarchy that attracts our notice is that of Affyria; the firft, that is, that attempted to aggrandize itfelf by extenfive conquefts, and to fubjugate to its power the widely extended provinces of Afia; and the monarchs of Affyria, whether they weilded the royal fceptre at Nineveh, or at Babylon, neither purfued their conquefts to any confiderable diftance, nor retained them long in quiet and fecure poffeffion: " fwift and impetuous in their careers as the eagle[c]," to ufe the emblem of the Prophet, they

[c] Dan. vii. 4.

were continually losing the advantages which they had gained: the universal monarchy, at which they aspired, they never in reality possessed; and they may be said rather to have been continually contending for it, than to have enjoyed it under any fixed and settled form. Often they were the agents of God, to punish his chosen people for their disobedience: and the glory and power of their dominion was at its height when they had carried the tribes of Israel and Judah into captivity. But in the pride of their hearts they attributed to themselves the glory which belonged to God; and while they were acting as the appointed ministers of his vengeance, they fondly thought that they were promoting the schemes of their own ambition. "Howbeit," says the Prophet, speaking of the Assyrian, "he meaneth not so, neither doth his heart think so; for it is in his heart to destroy and cut off nations not a few: for he saith, by the strength of my hand I have done it, and by my wisdom, for I am prudent, and I have removed the bounds of the people, and have robbed their treasures, and I have put down the inhabitants

SERMON VII.

tants like a valiant man[d]." But the Almighty punifhed this idle boafting, he brought to nought the counfels of the ambitious, he numbered their kingdom, and finifhed it; and he gave up Babylon, the " glory of kingdoms, and the beauty of the Chaldees excellency[e]," as he had given up Nineveh before it, to become a defolation without an inhabitant. Thus it may be obferved how clofely and intimately the fortunes of the other nations of mankind were connected with thofe of the people of God: Babylon was to be deftroyed for the defolation which it had brought upon Jerufalem; and the chofen fervant of God, who was at once announced by the Prophet as the deftroyer of the Aflyrian monarchy, and the deliverer of the Jewifh nation, was alfo to become the founder of a new empire, more extenfive, and more powerful far, than the former.

The founder of the Perfian monarchy was endowed by God with a more than ordinary fhare of talents and of virtues, and bleft with a conftant feries of victories and

[d] Ifai. x. 7—13.   [e] Ifai. xiii. 19.

prosperity. " The Lord of Israel," says he, in the decree which he issued for the restoration of the Jews, " the Lord of Israel, the most high Lord, has made me King of the whole world[f]." Coming forth from a poor and barren country, and inured from his earliest childhood to toils and hardship, he became, under the protection of the Almighty, the sovereign of a powerful empire, whose boundaries to the East and West were the Indus and the Ægean Sea; to the North, the Caspian and the Euxine; and to the South, Ethiopia and the Arabian Gulph. Under the dominion of his successors, the Asiatic empire of the Persians was enlarged and confirmed: but all their attempts to subjugate the nations of Europe were fruitless; the time for uniting the two continents under the same dominion was not yet arrived.

It is one of the most curious and instructive lessons in the history of mankind, to observe with what unerring certainty the ambition of the Persian monarchs, and their eager desire to subdue the free re-

[f] 2 Chron. xxxvi. 22. Ezra i. 2.

publics

publics of Greece, terminated in their own destruction; to mark how the restless spirit of those turbulent democracies, their jealousy and hatred of each other, and their own internal dissensions, reduced them to submit at last to a foreign yoke; and then to notice how the accomplishment of their long projected vengeance upon their eastern enemies was reserved for him whom God had chosen to be the conqueror of Asia. Of that extraordinary person, whose brilliant atchievements have been at all times the constant theme of undistinguishing panegyric, I have only to remark, that, in obeying the dictates of his own inordinate ambition, he carried on the general design of Providence; that with wisdom to devise, and vigour and promptitude to execute, any project of conquest, of whatever extent or magnitude it might be, there is scarcely a doubt, humanly speaking, but that he would have become in reality, what his flatterers and panegyrists have called him, the master of the world; that he would have opened a secure and easy communication between the several nations of his vast empire; that he would have

con-

connected them by alliances and intermarriages, have enriched them by commerce, and perhaps have polished and refined them by arts and literature. But the hour was not yet arrived; and it pleased the Almighty to cut off this mighty conqueror in the very prime of his life, and in the full career of his victories. It was not, however, by his own premature death alone, that the vices of Alexander, his pride, his intemperance, and his sanguinary cruelty received their punishment; the just vengeance of God pursued him to the ruin of his house, and the destruction of all his dearest connections. The extensive dominions, which his prowess had acquired, were split and divided, as the Prophet of God had declared that they should be; and the endless disputes and dissensions of his successors converted the world into a theatre of war and bloodshed, and desolated the fairest provinces of Europe and Asia. In the mean time, that people, for whom God had destined the sovereignty of the universe, had been gradually increasing in strength and consequence; the valour of their soldiers, and the wisdom of their senators, had been uni-

uniformly directed from the very first dawn of their power, to the aggrandizement of their territories. No opportunity was ever lost, no means were neglected, either in peace or war, by open force, by stratagem, or by alliance, of extending the boundaries of their dominion; and they were now in a situation to avail themselves of those distractions, which convulsed the empire of Macedon.

To trace the progress of the Roman power, until its favourite object of universal empire was obtained, would be to detail a trite and well known story; and the fact of its having obtained it, is all that is necessary for me to insist upon at present. "Macedon," says an historian, who flourished in the days of the empire, "never did reduce the world to obedience; for neither did it possess all Africa, nor all Europe. But Rome does rule over all the earth as far as it is inhabited; and all the sea, not only the Mediterranean, but also the ocean as far as it is navigable; having first and alone, of all the celebrated kingdoms
of

of the earth, made the East and West the bounds of its empire [g]."

Thus we have seen that the uniform plan of Providence was preserved throughout; that the Monarchs of the East, although they styled themselves the Lords of the universe, and, in the hyperbolical language of their country, were used to addrefs their public decrees to all nations, people, and languages upon earth, were in reality limited to their Asiatic poffeffions; and that every attempt to extend their dominion, and to establish an universal empire, was checked and retarded, until the appointed time was come; and the people, for whom this dominion was reserved, were able to acquire and maintain it.

It remains only briefly to consider, in what way the subjection of the world to one government tended to promote the interests of Christianity.

Christianity, as I have said above, was to

[g] Dionyf. Halicarn. Antiq. Rom. lib. i. p. 3. Edit. Hudson.

be propagated by human means, by argument, by perfuasion, by a fair and candid addrefs to the underftandings of mankind; and this appeal was to be made perfonally by thofe, to whom the bleffed Author of our faith had committed that important office.

Now if the feveral nations, to whom the Gofpel was preached, had been unknown to each other; if there had been no connection or intercourfe between them; if their governments had been hoftile to each other, it is fcarcely poffible to conceive, how the Apoftles could have executed their tafk, unlefs indeed we fuppofe the interpofition of Providence, by a continued miracle, diftinct from thofe miracles, which were the true and proper credentials of their miffion.

And if fuch a difficulty as this may be conceived to have exifted in the cafe of the Apoftles, of courfe it would have been greater in that of their fucceffors, when the extraordinary gifts of the Spirit were withdrawn, when the mighty fign and wonder no longer accompanied the teacher, but every thing was left to the exertions of human industry and abilities. But the Almighty provided for the safety of his infant Church, by deferring the appearance of its holy Founder, until such channels of communication had been opened, and till the preachers of righteousness could speak, in the name of the blessed Jesus, to every nation under Heaven.

It has been observed, and perhaps with reason, that, if Judea had not been a Roman province at the time of our Saviour's birth; if the Jews had not been subject to the jurisdiction of the Empire, and consequently enrolled in the general register of the imperial subjects, the prediction of the Prophet would not have been verified, "that out of Bethlem should come forth a Saviour, whose goings forth were from old, from everlasting [h]." It has also been observed, which is a point of still greater importance, that if there had not been a Roman Governor in Jerusalem, the Jewish Sanhedrim, by their own law, could not

[h] Mic. v. 2.

have

have condemned our blessed Redeemer to that death, which it was ordained that he should suffer as an atonement for the sins of Man.

If there be truth and reason in these remarks, they are an additional evidence of the goodness of God, who was continually watching over his creatures, and guiding their wayward and unsteady passions, by his unerring wisdom, to the minute accomplishment of his gracious purposes. But all that I have endeavoured to shew is, that the world was subjected to the dominion of Rome, in order to facilitate the promulgation of the Gospel.

The holy Prophet, from whose volume I have taken the words of my text, by the general tenor of his Prophecy, seems, if I do not mistake, to point to such a conclusion in those wonderful productions, which the venerable Mede has called " the sacred Calendar and Almanack of Prophecy:" it is easy to trace one great design throughout.

The four Monarchies are to rise in regular

lar fucceffion, to exceed each other in power and extent of territory; and the fourth is to furpafs the other three, and to poffefs the whole earth. But the Prophecy clofes not there: in the hallowed ftrain of infpiration, the Prophet goes on to paint the diffolution of this mighty Empire, the feveral parts into which it was to be broken, the fufferings of the true Church, and, finally, the everlafting kingdom of Chrift. We know that the remarkable predictions of the holy Daniel, which relate to events prior to the publication of Chriftianity, were fully confirmed; that the bittereft enemies of the Chriftian faith confeffed, that they were fo. We have a right therefore to conclude, that what relates to events fubfequent to that period will be verified alfo; and, with this reflection to cheer him, a Chriftian ought never to defpond. For whatever be the fate of earthly governments and human inftitutions; whatever be the fate even of thofe eftablifhments, by which human prudence hath cherifhed and fupported true Religion, we have a fure and certain hope, that Chrift at laft will be " all in all;" and under every diftrefs and

perfepersecution of this life, we may look forward with confidence to that awful moment, which the Prophet, in his magnificent language, has taught us to expect; " when the Son of man shall come with the clouds of Heaven; and he shall come to the *Ancient of Days*; and there shall be given to him dominion and glory, and a kingdom, that all people, nations, and languages, should serve him; his dominion is an everlasting dominion, which shall not pass away, and his kingdom, that which shall not be destroyed[i]."

[i] Dan. vii. 13, 14.

SERMON VIII.

GALATIANS iv. 4.

WHEN THE FULNESS OF TIME WAS COME, GOD SENT FORTH HIS SON.

ST. Paul, throughout the whole of his Epistle to the converts of Galatia, is taking pains to warn them against the artifices of those false teachers, who wished to impose upon them the work of the Levitical ceremonies: " There was a time," he says, " when those ceremonies were necessary; when the rite of circumcision, the attendance at the stated festivals of the Jewish Church, and the observance of the Sabbatical years, were not only allowable, but obligatory;" but that all those ordinances, which, in fact, were nothing more than faint and partial representations of the truth, were now at an end, for that " the fulness of time was come," when the Son of God had appeared to redeem those who were under the bondage of the law. This expression of the Apostle, " the fulness of time," which he uses upon other occasions, as well as in this address to the Galatians, may be understood in two ways; for it may either mean, that all the previous steps by which God had determined to open the way gradually for the final revelation of his will to man, were now completed, and that nothing more of preparation, or introduction, was necessary; or it may mean, that the period, at which our Saviour entered upon his ministry, was, from the existing circumstances of the world, the fittest that could have been devised for the publication of the Gospel.

What the preparations were, by which the great scheme of Providence was gradually conducted to its accomplishment, it has been the object of my former Discourses

courses to enumerate. We have seen, that a peculiar people were separated from the rest of mankind, to preserve the belief of the one true God; that a country of peculiar fertility was assigned to them for their residence; that God himself was their King; that while the ceremonies of their religion prescribed an outline, a shadow of the good things of which their future Messiah was to be the body and the substance; a succession of inspired Prophets from time to time unfolded the glorious plan of redemption, specified the season at which the Redeemer was to appear in mortal shape, and the nature of the sufferings which he was patiently to endure; and that, in order to secure the permanence of this preparatory system, for so long a time, at least, as its existence was necessary, the providence of God miraculously preserved the Jewish people, with their civil polity, and their religion, in the form originally delivered to them by their inspired Legislator; the rest of mankind, in the mean time, being brought, by the controul of God's providence, into that political situation, which was most likely to facilitate the general diffusion of the Gospel.

To assign the reason for every step in this gradual preparation, is a task beyond the reach of human abilities. In that one comprehensive plan, which extends from the very foundation of the world to the final consummation of all things, there must necessarily be many hidden motives, and many nice connections between the effect and its cause, which will elude the search of beings who see imperfectly, and know only in part: but even our limited knowledge, faint and imperfect as it is, enables us to pronounce, that had the Son of God come into the world at an earlier period of society, or without any previous introduction, the holy lessons which he taught, and gracious promises which he announced to man, would have died away, in the very infancy of their promulgation, unless we suppose, that human nature had been differently constituted; that the Creator had taken away from his creatures the power to will, and to act, and had interposed, by a constant miracle, displayed in every part of the universe, to teach mankind his will, and to enforce obedience to it.

And if on this account we can judge of

of the necessity of the preparation, it is also within the compass of our knowledge to judge of its effect—so that we have only to appeal to the evidence of facts: for it is an historical fact, that when our Lord came into the world, he did actually find the chosen race of Abraham, amidst the errors and corruptions of Idolatry, still worshipping " the one true God," " the God of their fathers," in the very form, and with the very ceremonies, which Moses their Lawgiver, by the command of God, had prescribed to them. He found them also waiting, with the most anxious solicitude, for his appearance: for while the impious scoffer ventured to accuse the Almighty of slowness and forgetfulness, in the execution of his promise, all pious and devout persons, like " the aged Simeon," and " the daughter of Phanuel," were looking for the consolation of Israel, in the full confidence, that, whatever might be the cause of so long a delay, God had not forgotten the promise of redemption, which had so often been repeated to their fathers.

The whole of Judea indeed, Herod, and all

all Jerusalem with him, was troubled, when the birth of the holy Jesus at Bethlehem was announced; ἐταράχθησαν, is the very strong expression, which the Evangelist uses; they were thrown into an agitation: some, no doubt, dreading the power of that glorious Person, who at length was come to rule over them; others anticipating the splendour of his victories, and the unlimited extent of his dominions; and perhaps the few of better minds and juster expectations, looking forward with delight to a reign of peace, and equity, and righteousness. Nor were these expectations confined to the Jews: it was a current opinion, derived unquestionably from the Prophecies of Holy Writ, that about this period of time an extraordinary Person would appear in the East; that he would be a powerful and mighty Prince, and would subject all the nations of the earth to his dominion.

The same Prophecies, which raised the expectation of the Messiah, furnished the means of knowing him, when he actually came: it was natural to expect, that impostors

postors would avail themselves of this general eagerness; that, under the glorious title of the promised Deliverer, they would summon their countrymen to their standard; and would attempt to acquire power and opulence for themselves, under the specious pretext of rescuing their country from the Roman yoke. God therefore had given his people infallible criteria, by which they were to distinguish their Messiah from all such false Christs, and false Prophets. Was he of the tribe of Judah, and of the lineage of David? Was he born at Bethlehem? Could he control or suspend the operations of nature; restore sight to the blind, and vigour and activity to the cripple? Did he know all things? Could he penetrate the secret thoughts of the human heart, and unfold the hidden events of futurity? These were tests, by which, not only men of education and learning, the chief Priest and the Scribe, but the illiterate descendant of Abraham, in whatever situation of life he was placed, had been taught to distinguish the character of their Christ.

So

So far then it may be said, that the "fulness of time was come;" because it was the time which the Holy Spirit had fixed, for the appearance of the great Deliverer of mankind; because he was universally expected; and because all the methods, by which God thought fit to prepare for his approach, had been brought to full maturity. These, however, are the reasons, why God did not send forth his Son at an earlier period. But to know why this period was fitter for his appearance than any other would have been, why a farther delay would not have been practicable, consistently with the merciful design of improving the moral condition of mankind, and fitting them for the enjoyment of everlasting happiness; to understand "the fulness of time" in this sense, it will be necessary to consider, what really was the state of mankind, when the Saviour of the world entered upon his public ministry, and what they actually knew of their duty to God, and to each other. When the holy Forerunner of the Messiah announced to his countrymen the speedy approach of the kingdom of Heaven, and warned them to

save

SERMON VIII.

save themselves from future misery, by a timely repentance, the general depravity of mankind, both of Jews and Gentiles alike, was at its height; a depravity, which pursued its course without any check or control; for they who wished to stem the torrent, had not the power of doing it; they had no barrier to obstruct its progress, nothing but a vague, speculative morality, and a nominal religion, without any real influence upon the heart, or the understanding.

The Jews (for I will first consider the circumstances of the Jewish Church), the Jews, from the time of their captivity in Babylon, had been punctual in their observance of the Mosaic Law; that is, they had never relapsed into that Idolatry, of which their forefathers had been guilty. Whether it was, that the remembrance of former sufferings had taught them to conquer their natural propensity to adopt the vices of their neighbours, or that the most corrupt and the most vicious did not return with their brethren to the land of promise, or that the nearer approach of the
great

great Redeemer kept them in continual awe and suspense; whatever was the real cause, the fact is undoubted, that at no period of their history were the Jews so tenacious of their own law, or so free from the base and abominable contamination of Idol worship.

But it does not follow, because they had less Idolatry, that they had therefore more true Religion; the very reverse of this was in fact the case. Worshippers of the one living God they certainly were; in the holy Temple of Jerusalem, however inferior it might be to the splendid fabric of Solomon, all the high solemnities of the Mosaic ritual were celebrated still in honour of the God of Israel: but the popular opinions of their God, the notions which were generally entertained of his nature and his attributes, were very unworthy of him. Accustomed, as they had been, to consider the Lord Jehovah as the tutelary God of their nation, the Jews confined to themselves all the benevolent acts of his Providence; and admitting that he was the Creator and the Governor of the universe,
they

SERMON VIII.

they still proudly and foolishly supposed, that they were the sole and exclusive objects of his paternal solicitude. Many of them had been taught to fix their minds upon symbolical representation of the Divine presence; and they were yet to learn, that the God of their fathers was a pure æthereal spirit, and that he was only " to be worshipped in spirit and in truth."

Followers of the Mosaic Law they were undoubtedly; but in the mode of observing its precepts, there was far more of superstition, than of true and sincere piety. Such of its minute ordinances as were instituted for temporary purposes, to wean them from their attachment to Egyptian superstitions, or to guard them from the abominations of the nations of Canaan, were now of little avail; and, without any prejudice to their religion, might have sunk into total disuse. But those the bigotted Jew esteemed as highly as the weightier matters of the Law; as the necessary ceremonies of his ritual, or the important obligations of the Decalogue; while the rulers of synagogues, the guides

and

and inſtructors of the people, ſo far from correcting their errors, impoſed upon them an additional weight of ceremonies, and required them to pay the ſame obedience to their own abſurd traditions, as they did to the ſacred mandates of the Law and the Prophets.

That the Moſaic Law in its beſt ſtate, and when entirely free from the gloſſes and fanciful additions of the Cabbala, was defective in many points, cannot be denied, and it had the defect neceſſarily belonging to it, as a preparatory diſpenſation. The Law made nothing perfect, but was the introduction of a better hope: it was a partial law, ſuited to the circumſtances of one particular people alone, and limiting its ſervices to a particular place. It permitted, if it did not ſanction, acts, which natural reaſon diſapproves, and which the law of univerſal righteouſneſs poſitively forbids; and paſſed over others in total ſilence, which this latter and more perfect law enjoins as duties. As a ritual worſhip, its true and only uſe was, to preſerve the people from the contagion of idolatry, and,

by

SERMON VIII. 223

by the ufe of expiatory facrifices, to accuftom them to the idea of vicarious punifhment, and to prepare their minds for the great Chriftian doctrine of atonement to be made for the fins of man by the blood of the Redeemer. As a rule of focial duty between man and man, it was incomplete, becaufe, although it checked and repreffed the inordinate affections of man, and forbad all flagrant violations of moral juftice; yet we try in vain to find in it the duties of mutual forbearance, or forgivenefs of injuries, of lowlinefs of mind, of patience, humility, and all enduring charity.

Fully competent therefore, as it was, to anfwer the purpofes which God defigned it to anfwer, as a law of general obligation it was materially imperfect: it neither taught men their duty to each other, nor qualified them for acceptance, and pardon with God: it was, as the Apoftle calls it, "a miniftry of death and condemnation [a], a fubjection to a curfe [b], a killing letter [c]."

[a] 2 Cor. vii. 9.   [b] Gal. ii. 13.   [c] 2 Cor. iii. 6.

But

But the Law, faulty as it was in itself, was rendered still more so by the corruptions, which the Jews themselves had introduced into it, by the disputes of their sectaries, and the chimerical inventions of their Rabbins.

At the head of their Church were the Pharisees, a corrupt and odious sect, whose principles and conduct are uniformly marked by our blessed Lord with the severest terms of reproach. With all the external appearance of sanctity; with a pious demeanor, and an ostentatious parade of devotion in public; the Pharisee had only the semblance of piety, without any real purity of heart, or any proper sense of religious duties: in his ideas, minute attention to dress, to his prayers, and his phylacteries; the exact performance of the legal ablutions, and a scrupulous observance of the holy day of rest, were more than sufficient to compensate for the neglect or the violation of the great obligations of morality. That he should be called into another existence after this life, he did believe; but of future judgment, or future retribution, he seems to have had no expec-

expectation. His foul, he thought, after death, would reanimate fome other body, diffcrent from his, and totally unconnected with it. Conceiving therefore, as he did, that all merit confifted in the punctual performance of ceremonies, and that that alone would entitle him to the favour of God, beneath the fpecious mafk of piety and devotion, he concealed a corrupt heart, a depraved and fenfual appetite, and a temper morofe, unforgiving, and uncharitable.

The Sadducee, on the other hand, the rival and opponent of the Pharifee in the purfuit of worldly ambition, was the decided enemy of thofe traditions, which the other prized fo highly; he adhered ftrictly and literally to the written precepts of his Divine Legiflator. But then he did not fee, as he might have feen, in the facred Volume of his religion, any intimations whatever of a future life: all his views, and all his expectations, were limited to the prefent world: the rewards which he hoped to receive, if he obeyed the commandments of his law, were power, and wealth, and temporal profperity; and the only punifhment nishment which he dreaded was the loss of worldly advantages, of rank, of opulence, or popular reputation.

Under the guidance of such instructors as these were, without a Prophet to censure their vices, and to call them to repentance, their God not interfering, as he had done in the days of their ancestors, to check the progress of iniquity by immediate punishment, the Jewish nation gradually rose to such an enormous pitch of profligacy and wickedness, that, as their own historian confesses (and surely he cannot be accused of want of partiality for his countrymen), if the Romans had delayed to strike the blow, God would have punished them by an earthquake, or a pestilence, or perhaps have poured down upon them, in fire, the fury of his vengeance, as he did in early days upon the guilty cities of Sodom and Gomorrah [d].

Let us now turn from the Jews to the Gentile world, and see whether the Heathen, when the Gospel of righteousness was

[d] See Josephus Antiq.

offered to him, poffeffed any knowledge of religious duty, or any moral law, which the Jew had not.

It had pleafed the Almighty, for what reafon it would be folly and prefumption in man to enquire—but it had pleafed the Almighty "to wink at," "ὑπεριδεῖν," to overlook the times of Gentile ignorance: the whole race of mankind, with the exception of the chofen people of Ifrael, had been left to the guidance of the unwritten law implanted by the Creator in the hearts of all his creatures, and to the feeble light which they could derive from the corrupt traditions of primitive revelations.

Whatever effect the law of nature, or the light of reafon, might have had upon the few, who could think and reafon, it never can be fuppofed to have had any practical influence upon the great mafs of mankind. The popular fyftems of Heathen mythology, and the ceremonies of Heathen worfhip, inftead of purifying the heart, and correcting the evil propenfities of human nature, were, in fact, a fertile fource of error

ror in opinions, and profligacy in practice. Corrupt and diffolute manners, the open violation of decency, and the fhamelefs indulgence of licentious paffions, were the fatal but neceffary confequences of the exhibitions, the fhews, and the feftivals, which the ritual of Polytheifm required. The temples of their Gods were too often the fcene of the moft fcandalous exceffes, while the delufions of their Oracles, which were now become a conftant theme of ridicule, and the artifices of their Priefthood, which the man of letters delighted in expofing to the vulgar, gradually inclined them to doubt the reality of what they had been taught; to think that there was no fuch Being exifting as a God, and that the whole fabric of Religion was a fyftem of falfehood, the invention of artful ftatefmen and politicians.

Thus then, faid the freethinker, meaning to infinuate that the Chriftian Revelation could not be neceffary, the evil of Polytheifm corrected itfelf: but how did it correct itfelf? By creating in the mind a general indifference to all religion whatfoever: and it would be a difficult tafk to fhew, that

that mankind would have been better, or happier, had Atheism been substituted in the place of Polytheism.

But was there no check to be found then, or no controul, to resist the torrent of impiety? Could not the light of reason teach men to subdue the lawless violence of their passions? And had not philosophy sufficiently investigated the proper motives of human conduct, and fixed a certain and unerring rule of moral obligation?

Far be it from me wantonly to depreciate the labours of the illustrious few, who quitted the abstruse researches of metaphysics, for the more plain and more useful investigation of moral duty; who taught that there was a Supreme God, by whose power the world was created, and by whose Providence it was governed; that man, as a social being, was to consider the utility and the happiness of the community to which he belonged, as the rule of his conduct; that the soul of man was immortal and immaterial; and that, after the dissolution of the body, it would still have life and vigour,

vigour, and continue to exist in another state.

Sacred be the memory of those, who, after they had pursued their inquiries as far as it was possible for unassisted reason to go, with the humility of real science, scrupled not to aver their ignorance: the best and the wisest of them declared, that none but a teacher from Heaven could remove his doubts; and had it been his fortune to have heard the admirable wisdom of that blessed Teacher, he would have been amongst the foremost to hail with joy the dawn of so glorious a day: before the pure and perfect wisdom of the Gospel he would have cast down all the unprofitable theories, the high imaginations, and the idle boastings of human reason, and have acquiesced with gratitude in the revealed will of God.

Unfortunately, however, the influence of the best philosophy was confined to the few who professed it, and to their immediate followers. Truths, which are only to be learnt by a regular deduction of reason, are not calculated for common minds; the

fairest

SERMON VIII.

faireft ideal pictures of virtue, however juft, or however beautiful they might be, had no allurement for the generality of mankind; and even the hope, or the expectation, of a future exiftence was of little real fervice, when it was a matter of doubt, whether the foul, after its feparation from the body, was to be confcious of what had been done in that body or not; whether it was to be loft in the immenfity of the Deity, from whom it originally emanated; or to be joined to another body, and to repeat the fame viciffitudes of acting and fuffering upon earth, in endlefs revolutions.

If fuch was the inefficacy of thofe fyftems, which alone deferve the name of philofophy, what was to be expected from the croud of difputants, who contended for fame and victory, and not for truth; from thofe who could juftify by arguments the worft excelfes, or thofe who maintained, that all actions were equally indifferent; that nothing in nature was either good or bad; and that vice and virtue were diftinctions invented by man, and only to be found in the inftitutions of human policy?

Or what reason was there to suppose, that the morals of the vulgar would be reformed, when the practice of the very philosophers themselves was continually at variance with their principles; when they, who inculcated a contempt of riches and honours, were eager to gratify the pursuits of worldly ambition; when the teacher of humility was notorious for his pride; and the advocate of temperance indulged in all the excesses of the grossest sensuality?

In such a painful state of uncertainty, unable to comprehend the principles of the true philosophy, and perplexed and bewildered by the intricate subtleties of the worst, the generality of mankind eagerly attached themselves to that sect, which promised to satisfy their scruples, and to allay their fears. That they would emancipate mankind from the shackles of superstition, would empower them to think and act for themselves, and teach them the true use of their reason, was the specious boast of Epicurus and his school; and this glorious liberty was to be acquired by the rejection of all those great truths, which
were

SERMON VIII.

were the cement of human fociety, and the foundation of all our happinefs.

The Epicurean had no God, or if he had a God, it was a God without a Providence; a God, flumbering in eafe and indolence, and carelefs of the fate of the wretched mortals, who were to wander at will, amidft the cares, the perplexities, and the dangers of their exiftence upon earth: and without the belief of a God, he had no idea of moral refponfibility, and no expectation of future judgment.

In his intercourfe with mankind, all his views, and all his motives, terminated in felf; his own profit, and his own pleafure, were the only incitements, that could roufe him into activity: and neither friendfhip, nor good faith, nor juftice, were regarded any farther than as they contributed to promote his intereft, or to gratify his pleafure.

This was the prevailing fyftem of the times; it was the fafhionable Philofophy, which all defcriptions of men began to admire, and to adopt: to the vulgar and the illiterate,

literate, it offered the enticing prospect of freedom from all restraint, and emancipation from all obligation; to the learned and the wealthy, it recommended itself, by the elegant manners of those who professed it, by the charms of beautiful poetry, and the refined voluptuousness which it justified and recommended.

Thus, if Philosophy had been permitted to take its course, instead of improving and cultivating the light of nature, it would have extinguished it entirely; it would have robbed its votaries of all that could make them virtuous or happy; and have plunged the miserable race of man into the thick and gloomy darkness of Atheism. But at this period precisely, when the world was almost without religion; when the Jew had nearly lost the spirit of the Mosaic Law, and corrupted the letter of it by his fanciful interpretations; and the Gentile, by his false philosophy, had thrown a mist over the feeble light of natural reason—at this period, " God sent forth his Son, to teach the way to righteousness," and " to awaken sinners to repentance."

Surely

SERMON VIII.

Surely then we cannot but admire the wifdom of God, and adore his goodnefs with humble gratitude, for fending into the world the Heavenly Inftructor whom he had promifed, at the very moment that his inftructions were moft neceffary to the happinefs of his creatures.

But if the neceffity of a better guide and a wifer teacher was admitted, how did it happen, that when a Teacher came, calling himfelf the Son of God, and proving his title by miracles—how did it happen, that the Jews rejected, and perfecuted even unto death, the very Perfon whom they had fo long expected; and that the Gentiles, above all, the rich, the powerful, and the learned, who ought to have been amongft the earlieft converts, treated the Religion, which he offered them, with fcorn and derifion, and purfued his followers with the bittereft malignity? Is not this a proof, fays the unbeliever, either that he was not in reality the Perfon whom he profeffed to be; or that his doctrines did not contain the leffons of wifdom and righteoufnefs, which we maintain they did?

The

The fact is undoubted; but the inference, which the Sceptic would draw from it, by no means follows: on the contrary, the conquest which Christianity obtained over the obstacles, by which its enemies tried to retard its progress, is in itself the strongest proof, that it really was the word of God.

The general depravity of the times, the decay of all practical Religion, and the want of proper criteria, by which to distinguish right from wrong, created prejudices against the Gospel of Christ, which were common to all mankind, to Jew and Gentile alike. The very first awakening call to repentance, by which the harbinger of the Messiah had proclaimed his near approach, contained a command, to which minds hardened in wickedness, and accustomed to the uncontrouled indulgence of their passions, could not immediately reconcile themselves. But when the holy Teacher appeared himself in person, they found, that the whole system of his Religion was founded upon this doctrine of repentance; that, in order to become his disciples, and to share the rewards of his king-

SERMON VIII.

kingdom, they muſt abandon, without delay, all their habitual indulgences; they muſt renounce and execrate the vices which they had practiſed with impunity, and with humble and ſincere contrition muſt confeſs their own unworthineſs, and their utter inability to obtain ſalvation, without the free grace and pardon of God.

From ſo humiliating a confeſſion, the pride of the Jewiſh Teacher and the Gentile Sophiſt revolted at once: in the mean time their appropriate characters, and their reſpective ſituations, gave them other prejudices, and other prepoſſeſſions, peculiar to each.

The Jew had always miſunderſtood the promiſe originally made to the Patriarch, and repeated continually by every one of the inſpired Prophets. He had accuſtomed himſelf, as is well known, to expect not a Spiritual deliverer, or a Spiritual kingdom; but a mighty Prince, and an earthly Sovereignty. Ever inclined to faction and ſedition, and uneaſy under the dominion of Rome, the Jewiſh people looked for a
leader,

leader, who would drive out the imperial legions from Jerusalem, and extend his conquests far beyond the confines of the Holy Land. All their ambitious views therefore, were demolished at once, when they saw the Person, who announced himself as the Christ, entering the holy city; not with the splendid pageant of a conqueror, but "meek, and lowly, and sitting upon an ass [d]." All their dreams of conquest and dominion vanished, when they saw, that, instead of calling his followers to a military standard, or animating them with the hope of that liberty, for which they pined, his time was passed in healing the sick, and cheering the unhappy; in dictating to the poor and the lowly the plain and easy lessons of his pure morality; and promising even to publicans and sinners, the blessed fruits of repentance, and the glorious hope of eternal life. And all the visionary schemes of grandeur and power faded away before them, when they found, that, to obtain an inheritance in his kingdom, they must quit the possession of worldly honours and worldly riches; must for-

---

[d] Matth. xxi. 5.

sake

SERMON VIII.

fake their kindred, their families, and their friends, and become the poor and perfecuted followers of a defpifed Nazarite.

The Jew had alfo been taught to expect, that his Law would be perpetual; that its ceremonies were of univerfal obligation; and that the holy Temple of Jerufalem, in the days of the Meffiah, would be thronged with fuppliants from all the nations under heaven. He was perfuaded alfo that falvation belonged exclufively to himfelf, and was to be obtained only by the punctual obfervance, not of the Mofaic ritual merely, but of all the frivolous ceremonies, which the Scribe and Pharifee had ingrafted upon it. What then was his furprife, his mortification, and his refentment, when he heard from the mouth of our bleffed Lord, that his kingdom was referved not for thofe who purified their bodies by ablutions, but for the pure in heart; when he faw him, as he thought, violating the Law, and defpifing the Sabbath, and declaring, in juftification of his practice, that " God would have mercy, and not judgment!" What was his indignation, when he heard, that

the

the Apostles were commissioned to announce " the tidings of salvation to all nations" indiscriminately, and to declare, that God was not to be adored in this or that particular place, but that the reasonable service of the heart might be offered to him in every climate, and by every created being!

To the anger, which the defeat of their fondest hopes, and the loss of their favourite projects, excited in the nation at large, the leaders of the people, the chief Priests and Elders, the Scribes and Pharisees, added a peculiar spirit of resentment and revenge against the practice of our blessed Lord; for he had unmasked their hypocrisies, and exposed their vices to the multitude: thus they all conspired to execute the eternal purpose of God—for " of a truth, Lord," says the sacred historian, " against thy holy child Jesus, whom thou hast anointed, the people of Israel were gathered together, for to do whatsoever thy hand and thy counsel determined before to have done [e]."

[e] Acts iv. 27.

SERMON VIII.

The Gentile, to the prejudice which he had in common with the Jew, added alfo particular prepoffeffions of his own: whilft the corruption of his morals, his profligacy, and his wickednefs, rendered him equally averfe to a Religion of purity, of conftraint, and felf-denial, his indifference and careleffnefs about all religions prepoffeffed him againft that, which claimed an exclufive preference above all others. Chriftianity, in his idea, was a gloomy, unfocial fyftem of Atheifm; for the followers of Chrift declared, that they would hold no fellowfhip or correfpondence with the works of darknefs; that the idols of Paganifm were an abomination; and that it was an impious act even to enter the Temples confecrated to the impure divinities.

To the proud Sophift, it was a thing ftrange and incredible, that a God had appeared upon earth, in a ftate of poverty and humiliation, and had fubmitted to a painful and ignominious death; that the perfons, whom he had appointed to diffeminate the precepts of his Religion, were not men of learning and education; not Philofophers,

sophers, but plain, unlettered Fishermen; and that the histories, which recorded his actions, and his discourses, were written in a simple, inartificial method, without any of the graces of style, or composition.

The magistrate and the statesman meanwhile dreaded the introduction of a new Religion, which tended immediately to effect a change in all the customs and habits of life, and to overthrow all the rites and ceremonies, which long practice had established.

Thus it appears, that they, who rejected the desire of all nations when he came, were influenced by their own corruption, and their own fatal prepossession; and it is, as I observed before, an incontestible evidence of the truth of our holy Faith, that it triumphed over all those obstacles; that, in spite of distress and persecution, the number of its converts increased continually; and that, in God's good time, it became the established belief of the Gentiles.

Still,

SERMON VIII.

Still, fays the adverfary of our Faith, granting its progrefs, what were its effects? Did it really accomplifh the purpofe for which, you fay, it was providentially introduced at that particular period of time? Did it inftruct mankind in their duties to God, and to each other? And are men wifer and better now, than they were before the eftablifhment of the Chriftian Faith?

Now in order to determine, with fairnefs and candour, what the efficacy of Chriftianity really has been, and to afcertain, as far as we are permitted, why it has not been greater, we muft recollect what was the real defign of its inftitution, and what was its true character.

Chriftianity profeffes to give mankind a moral Law, for the regulation of their conduct in this life; and to point out to them the means, by which they are to obtain everlafting happinefs in another.

Whether the moral Law be not as perfect as it is poffible for us to conceive;

whe-

whether it does not far surpafs all the fyftems of Ethics, which human reafon had framed, and all the precepts, which God had before vouchfafed to reveal, it is eafy to determine, by opening the facred volumes of the Evangelifts and the Apoftles: there we find " a new commandment," delivered to us by the blefled Jefus, " that we love one another." There we find that humility, meeknefs, moderation, forbearance, and charity, are the virtues, which can alone make us happy in ourfelves, or ufeful to our fellow-creatures. There too we find that the evil inclination, the rifing wifh, and the fecret intention to fin, are as guilty in the fight of God as the criminal act itfelf.

Such then being the morality of the Gofpel, falvation and future happinefs are offered to us, after a virtuous and religious life; not in confequence of our merit, but as the free and voluntary gift of God, obtained for us by the precious blood of our Redeemer.

This fyftem, in both its parts, is offered to our acceptance; our affent to it is not extorted

SERMON VIII.

extorted from us; we are required to examine its evidences, and to receive it upon conviction; it is offered to us therefore, as beings refponfible for our opinions and our actions; and it leaves us, as it found us, free agents: we may therefore miftake or mifinterpret its doctrines, from ignorance or from prejudice, or, from the ungoverned impetuofity of paffion, we may tranfgrefs its plaineft commands.

If then the efficacy of Chriftianity has been partial, let the fault reft with man, and not with God; and let us not dare impioufly to arraign the juftice or the mercy of the Creator, becaufe his creatures have not profited, as they ought, by the falutary leffons, which he has given them: at the fame time, it cannot be denied, but that the real and pofitive efficacy of Chriftianity has been very confiderable. If we look to the earlieft period of its promulgation, the morals of the earlieft converts, the unexampled purity of their lives, and the fteady fortitude, with which they fubmitted to perfecution, to tortures, and to death, while they evince the fincerity of their

their belief, at the same time, are a decisive proof of the strong influence of their religion upon their minds.

If we trace the course of civilization, we shall find, that the progress of Christianity has ever been accompanied by progressive reformation, and improvement in the laws, the literature, and the manners of mankind. It was the mild and peaceable spirit of the Gospel, that stopped the sanguinary sports, which, with all their boasted refinement, the nations of antiquity delighted to behold: it was the same spirit, that checked the wanton barbarity, with which the master was authorised to tyrannize over his slave: it is the same spirit, that has mitigated the grievousness of war, and taught contending nations, that a state of warfare need not impede the exercise of the duties of common humanity; that the extension of science, and the courtesy of individuals to each other, might still be maintained.

To the morality of the Gospel private life is indebted for all its comforts, and all its regulated enjoyments; and the sorrows, which

SERMON VIII.

which he cannot avoid, are comparatively light to a Chriftian, becaufe he has the bleffed hope of futurity before him; and under the unequal difpenfations of this life, he anticipates the time, when the Father of mankind will fummon all his creatures to judgment.

If then Chriftianity has already done fo much, it may fairly be prefumed, that it will do more; that its influence bears a proportion to its progrefs; and that, when its glorious light is diffufed impartially over the whole world, its efficacy will become complete. Then we may expect, that the ftormy paffions, which at prefent agitate and convulfe the moral world, will be hufhed into repofe, and the whole race of man will be knit together in the bonds of Chriftian charity, and univerfal love. Then all the imagery of the Prophets, and all their beautiful defcriptions, will be realized: " the wolf fhall dwell with the lamb, and the leopard fhall lie down with the kid; and the calf, and the young lion, and the fatling together, and a little child fhall lead them [f]." " The wildernefs and the fo-

[f] Ifai. xi. 6.

litary

litary place shall be glad; and the desert shall rejoice, and blossom as the rose [g]." "For judgment shall dwell in the wilderness, and righteousness remain in the fruitful field; and the work of righteousness shall be peace; and the effect of righteousness, quiet and assurance for ever [h]."

[g] Isai. xxxv. 1.   [h] Isai. xxxii. 16.

SERMON IX.

MATTHEW xxviii. 19.

GO YE THEREFORE, AND TEACH ALL NATIONS.

SUCH was the parting command, which the Son of God gave to thofe righteous perfons, who had been the companions of his miniftry, and to whofe guardianfhip he had committed his infant Church. " Go," faid he, " to every creature, without any diftinction or partiality, and preach to all the doctrines of repentance, and remiffion of fins:" and, that they might not be difcouraged by the difficulty of the tafk, he cheered them with the confolatory promife
of

of his constant assistance, for "Lo," said he, "I am with you alway to the end of the world."

From this command and this promise, it is evident, that the religion, which the Son of God came in "the fulness of time" to establish, was not like the law of Moses, or the superstition of Paganism, a partial, local, or temporary system of worship, but was designed to connect the whole race of man in one common faith, and to endure till the final dissolution of the world. Such was the language, in which the Holy Spirit had invariably spoke of that kingdom, which the Redeemer of mankind was to found; that it was to be universal in its extent, and perpetual in its duration: "in thee," said the Almighty, when he first announced to the Patriarchs the merciful design of redemption, which had been formed before the world began; "in thee, and thy seed, shall all the nations of the earth be blessed [a]." And as the scheme is gradually unfolded, as the intimations of future deliverance become more explicit, and the

[a] Gen. xii. 3.

delineation of the perfon and character of the Deliverer more minute, the religion which he was to preach is always characterized by the fame properties of univerfality and perpetuity.

"In Judah," fays the royal Pfalmift, alluding to the peculiarity of the Jewifh covenant, and the limitation of their worfhip to a particular country—" in Judah was God known, and his name was great in Ifrael;" "in Salem was his tabernacle, and his dwelling-place in Sion [b]." 'But not fo does he fpeak of the Meffiah; for God faid unto his Son, " I will give thee the Heathen for thine inheritance, and the utmoft parts of the earth for thy poffeffion." At one time we are told, in the figurative language of Prophecy, that in the laft days, " it fhall come to pafs, that the mountain of the Lord's houfe fhall be eftablifhed on the top of the mountains, and fhall be exalted above the hills, and all nations fhall flow unto it [c]." At another, that " there fhall be a root of Jeffe, which fhall ftand for an enfign to the people, and to it fhall

[b] Pfalm lxxvi. 1, 2.   [c] Ifai. ii. 2.

the nations seek [d]." Sometimes the prevalence of Christianity is spoken of by the Holy Spirit, as the establishment of the kingdom of the Lord: " all nations," it is said, " shall remember and turn unto the Lord, and all the kindreds of the nations shall worship before him, for the kingdom is the Lord's [e]." And sometimes in loftier strains the Prophet celebrates the extent and continuance of this empire: " the kingdom of God, it is called, and an everlasting dominion extended over all people, nations, and languages, that should not pass away, nor be destroyed [f]."

The Prophets therefore having taught us to expect, that Christianity would in God's good time become an universal Religion; and the blessed Jesus having directed his Apostles to publish the glad tidings of salvation to all mankind, how are we to account for its partial propagation, or why, it may be asked, at the present day, do we see the Jew still inflexibly adhering to his law, and the disciples of Mahomet still adoring the hallowed name of their false Prophet, whilst

[d] Isai. xi. 10.   [e] Psal. xxii. 27.   [f] Dan. vii. 14.

SERMON IX.

a confiderable part of the habitable world has never yet emerged from the dark and barbarous fuperftition of Paganifm?

It is natural, doubtlefs, for every reflecting mind, when it contemplates the moral and religious condition of man, to afk, why it is, that the truth hath been fo partially communicated? why it is, that fo many myriads of created beings are ftill permitted to continue in ignorance of thofe doctrines, which Chriftians maintain to be neceffary to the future falvation and happinefs of us all: and whether it be not reafonable to fuppofe, that before the clofe of feventeen centuries, " at the name of the holy Jefus, every knee would have bowed," and every tongue have confeffed the wonders of his love to man?

It will fcarcely be denied by any man, who hath ever opened the volume of our Faith, that Chriftianity, whether we confider it as a rule of moral obligation, or a ritual of religious fervice, or as the union of both, is far more calculated for general ufe, than any other religion that ever exifted

in

in the world. Let thofe who doubt it, compare the Gofpel of Chrift with the Law of Mofes, with the Koran of Mahomet, or with the multifarious fuperftitions of the Heathen; and then they will confefs the decided fuperiority of the Chriftian Law. The moral precepts of the Gofpel are adapted to every poffible variety of climates, of fituation, and of employment: they all flow from the fource of univerfal charity, that charity which teaches us, that as the children of one common parent, as fubject to the fame viciffitudes of mifery and happinefs here, and heirs of the fame immortality hereafter, we are to commiferate and relieve each other, to live for others more than for ourfelves, and to " do unto all men, as we would they fhould do unto us." The duty of prayer, the fecret unoftentatious worfhip of the heart, which God, under a former difpenfation, had declared to be more valuable and more pleafing to him than all the incenfe of facrifice and burnt-offering, and which Chrift enjoined by his precepts, and fanctioned by his practice—this great duty is as univerfally practicable, as it is univerfally obligatory.

The

SERMON IX.

The Chriftian is not called upon like the Jew of old, or the Mahometan of our days, to quit his ufual refidence, and his ordinary occupation, to traverfe diftant and inhofpitable countries, and to proftrate himfelf before the Altar of his God at a ftated feafon, and in a particular place; he is not burthened with a yoke of particular ceremonies, of periodical ablutions, which purify the body, but not the heart, or of minute and trifling obfervances, which vex and harrafs the mind, inftead of relieving and confoling it. The two fimple facraments, which mark the profeffion of his faith, interfere with no local duty, and interrupt none of the neceffary occupations of civil life: and his firft and earlieft leffon, to love his God, to believe in him, to ferve him, and to pray to him in fecret, it is eafy for him to practife at all times, and in all circumftances, in the place of his cuftomary refidence, in the bofom of his family, or in the private receffes of his clofet.

Thus, while the moral precepts and the religious exercifes of Chriftianity are adapted to the circumftances of every individual,

dividual, the religion itself, as a system, is compatible with every form of political society. While it is indeed the only basis upon which any government can exist with stability and firmness, it neither prescribes to man any particular form of government, nor refuses to connect itself with any. It gives the outline, the great and fundamental principles, upon which the very existence of civil society depends, moderation, good order, and submission to established authority: but it leaves to the wisdom of man to determine in what way those principles are to be applied; and what form of public institution is most congenial to his character and his circumstances, and most likely to ensure his happiness.

If then there be nothing in Christianity itself, to impede its progress; if, on the contrary, it addresses itself to all men alike, and is consistent with every possible form of civil community, this alone is a convincing proof, that the Omniscient Author of our faith originally designed it for the use and the comfort of all his creatures.

The

SERMON IX.

The Sceptic, the haughty Sophist, or the indifferent Polytheist, might indeed foolishly and ignorantly maintain, that the supreme Being did not require or expect uniformity of worship; nay, that he even took delight in the varied forms of devotion, which the ingenuity of his creatures devised, and the different and even contradictory opinions, which they formed of his nature and his attributes. But he, who believes that God is one, will instantly revolt from so monstrous an opinion; he will know, that the unity and simplicity of truth can alone be pleasing to Him; and that, as the Creator of the world, the Author of all good, and the benevolent Father of mankind, he cannot but choose to dispense his blessings with an impartial hand to all his creatures. It is on this ground, that we are at issue with the Deist: I admit, he would say, that if God were to communicate to man a system of religious belief, such as Christianity professes to be, we might conclude, as well from the nature of God, as from the character of the Religion, that all men would be Christians; that all would have heard the word and received it, it, and have embraced with joy the certain hope of everlasting life: but the fact is otherwise; therefore, his conclusion is, that because the Religion is not general, it is not the word of God.

Now, in the very principle of this objection, there seems to be at first sight a strange absurdity. If Christianity be not really a Divine revelation, if its morality be no better than human systems of ethics, if its promises of future life be delusive and false, why lament, that it is not communicated universally? If it be true, why call upon us to reject the precious gift of God, because there are persons existing in the world, to whom He has not yet vouchsafed to impart it?

To call the Almighty partial, is as absurd as it is impious; because whatever revelation of his will the Creator thinks fit to make, it must be, on his part, a free voluntary gift; the creature can have no right to demand it: and if it be not distributed in equal portions to all, we have no more right to murmur at the dispensations of

SERMON IX.

of God, than we have to complain, that all men are not precisely alike, that they have not the same health, the same strength, the same personal beauty, and the same mental endowments; that they were not placed higher in the scale of created beings, that they were not angels instead of men!

Is it not equally absurd and impious, to call the beneficent Author of our being unjust, when he himself hath condescended to tell us, that we should be tried, not only by what we know, but by what we are capable of knowing; that he will make allowances for want of talents, want of opportunities, and all the defects of unavoidable ignorance; and, as I had once before an occasion to observe, that the precious sacrifice of the Redeemer extends its influence to all mankind, even to those whom the day-spring from on high has never visited; " for thou wast slain," says the Apostle, " and hast redeemed us unto God by thy word, out of every kindred, and tongue, and people, and nation[g]." If then God hath voluntarily given us more than we have a right to

[g] Rev. v. 9.

ask, and hath declared, that he will not punish his creatures for an ignorance, which they cannot avoid, every suspicion of partiality or injustice is done away at once; and we have only to admire the mercy and the wisdom of God, in preserving throughout the uniform plan of gradual revelation, and in accommodating the holy lessons of his will to the circumstances and capacities of those who were to receive them.

God did not send forth his Son till " the fulness of time" arrived, till men felt their want of a guide and instructor from heaven, and were duly prepared to listen to his instruction. But the warning voice of the Almighty had not at any time been silent; God had spoken to his fallen creatures at " sundry times, and in divers manners;" he had promised in early times, that a Deliverer should one day come to rescue them from the dominion of sin: by his holy Prophets, he had repeatedly assured them, that the promise would be performed; and, as the appointed hour drew near, he had given clearer intimations of his

his design, and ampler descriptions of the nature of the deliverance, which they were to expect. Thus, the awful doctrine of redemption was unfolded by degrees, at distinct intervals of time, and only to one particular people, chosen by God, to be the guardian of his revelations. From all others it was purposely withheld; and even they, to whom the truth was revealed, neither felt its full value, nor comprehended its real purport.

If we turn to the prophetical descriptions of the Redeemer's kingdom, we find, that one of the marks, by which it is constantly characterised, is its gradual progress. This progress is represented under various images: sometimes the kingdom of heaven is a stone, which gradually becomes " a mountain, and fills the whole earth [h];" sometimes it is a tender plant, which, under the fostering hand of God, is reared to a fair and goodly tree. " I will take," saith the Lord God, " of the highest branch of the high cedar, and will set it; I will cut off from the top of his young twigs a tender

[h] Dan. ii. 35.

one, and will plant it upon a high mountain and eminent: in the mountain of the height of Ifrael will I plant it; and it fhall bring forth boughs, and bear fruit, and be a goodly cedar; and under it fhall dwell all fowl of every wing; in the fhadow of the branches thereof fhall they dwell[i]." Sometimes it is a " river whofe waters are at firft fhallow, till by degrees they rife to a great height, and become waters to fwim in, a river that cannot be paffed over [k]."

In ftrict conformity with thefe prophetical defcriptions of his kingdom, and with images of a fimilar nature, our bleffed Lord informs the Jews, that the kingdom of heaven will be progreffive, that its complete eftablifhment will not be immediate, but that it will advance from fmall beginnings, till it has poffeffed the whole earth. " The kingdom of heaven," fays he, " is like unto a grain of muftard feed, which indeed is the leaft of all feeds; but when it is grown, it is the greateft amongft herbs, and becometh a tree, fo that the

[i] Ezek. xvii. 22, 23.   [k] Ezek. xlvii. 5.

SERMON IX.

birds of the air lodge in the branches thereof¹."

It was the defign therefore of God, that Chriftianity fhould be progreffive, and that as its publication had been delayed until " the fulnefs of time" was come, fo its full and complete efficacy fhould be delayed, until the whole race of man were fully qualified to receive its faving truths. But here the queftion of the captious objector returns: Why was this progrefs neceffary? Could not the Gofpel have been preached at once in all places? and would it not have been better to have given to all men at once the opportunity of embracing it if they pleafed?

That God could have done this, had it fo feemed good to his eternal wifdom, cannot be denied, for " with God all things are poffible:" but then, we muft fuppofe a conftant miracle, or a miracle fo frequently repeated, that it would have ceafed to be a miracle, and would have loft all its force and efficacy, as an evidence of truth.

¹ Matt. xiii. 31. Mark iv. 31. Luk. xiii. 19

SERMON IX.

Upon no other fuppofition whatever, can we conceive the general diffufion of the great truths of Chriftianity, without any preparation, any previous moral difcipline, or any foundation of knowledge.

Follow the miffionary into the hut of the Indian, and obferve what a fruitlefs tafk it is to preach the crofs of Chrift crucified, to bid the favage repent, and confefs his fins, and be baptized into the faith of the blefied Jefus.

What impreffion can fuch a fummons make upon a mind that has never been taught to elevate its thoughts above the fenfible objects immediately before it? From the teacher of Heavenly truth he turns with contempt to the objects before him, to the glorious luminary, whofe fplendid orb he contemplates with aftonifhment, or even to the fhapelefs mafs of wood or stone, which he conceives to be the refidence of a Being fuperior in power to himfelf; who directs all the wonderful operations of nature, and rides in the ftorm and the whirlwind.

And

SERMON IX.

And can we expect in such circumstances to find converts, rational and sincere converts to the Christian faith? Or is it any impeachment of the authenticity or the truth of the Gospel, that when its doctrines have been preached to such hearers, they have either been unwilling to listen, or unable to comprehend them?

We who are Christians by education, who imbibe in our very infancy the first rudiments of our faith, who receive it as an impression upon our minds, long before we are capable of examining its evidences, and believing upon conviction, we are scarcely competent judges of the difficulty of preaching the faith of Christ to those who have every thing to learn, and who in some instances do not possess even the great fundamental truths of natural religion.

And it must be observed, that no argument, drawn from the conversion of the Gentiles in the Apostolic age, can be applicable to the propagation of the Gospel in these times. There is no similarity whatever between the two cases: that conversion

version was a miracle. The pride of learning, the obstinacy of ignorance, the fastidious contempt of the rich, and the sanguinary cruelty of the persecutor, all gave way before the irresistible force of truth. But why was this the case? It was because the Apostle went forth to execute his mission, under the immediate guidance of God. When he addressed the assemblies of the learned, the Holy Spirit gave him utterance, that he might confound the wisdom of the wise, and make vain the foolishness of men: and when he spoke to the ignorant multitude, the sign and the wonder accompanied his reasonings, and convinced them, that he was a messenger from God.

The Christian missionary has no such advantages: in the difficult and important enterprize of conversion, he has nothing to trust to but the powers of his own mind, assisted indeed, as we believe all good and pious designs will be assisted, by the ordinary grace of God, but without any of those gifts or graces, which were poured down so liberally from Heaven upon the chosen preachers of Christ. He has to argue,

gue, to perfuade, and if poffible to convince; but he cannot ftrike the minds of his hearers by a ftrain of infpired eloquence, nor overcome the ftubbornnefs of ignorance by a difplay of fupernatural power.

Surely then we may infer, that if the tafk of inftruction be committed merely to human agency, if all the extraordinary aids of the Spirit be withdrawn, fome previous knowledge muft be neceffary to form the mind of the convert; and want of civilization will be always an impediment to the general diffufion of the Chriftian Law.

This impediment it is eafy for man to fee, and perhaps it may be in the power of man to remove it. It is a natural obligation; natural reafon teaches us, that if we poffefs any knowledge, which is likely to improve the condition of our fellow creatures, or in any degree to promote their happinefs, we are bound to communicate it to them. In the cafe of religious inftruction, the command of our bleffed Lord to his Apoftles is binding upon every Chriftian, and every Chriftian may hope to receive

ceive the benefits of that gracious promise, that he would accompany and assist his faithful disciples in the execution of the trust committed to them, " even unto the end of the world."

If the attempt to diffuse the light of the Gospel more widely has not hitherto been attended with all the success that Christians could have wished, it by no means follows, that it will never succeed. The counsels of God are not to be measured by our impatience: the time, which to beings of so fleeting and transitory an existence as ours, appears to be of endless duration, to an eternal and infinite God is as nothing, a mere point in the boundless space of eternity; and, in the unsearchable ways of his providence, there may be numberless reasons for delay, which our feeble capacities cannot fathom.

We are not therefore to be discouraged, because the success of our endeavours has not been answerable to our hopes; and acting under the authority of a Divine command, we are not to suppose, as it has
some-

SERMON IX. 269

sometimes been foolishly argued, that it is wrong in man to try to hasten what God evidently purposes to retard; and it may be worth while to consider after all, whether we attribute our failure to its true cause. Do we know whether the motives of the teacher have always been pure, or the mode of his instruction always wise? In tracing the history of the attempts to propagate the Christian faith, have we not cause too often to lament, that the conqueror has forced his trembling captives reluctantly to take the baptismal vow, and that the emissary of the Papal see hath made the ministry of the Gospel subservient to the purposes of ambition, and discredited the sanctity of his religion, by accepting conditional vows, and partial confessions of the truth?

If the motive upon which we act be right, it can scarcely be doubted, whether we are performing an acceptable service to God or not. In attempting to diffuse the knowledge of his will, let no such groundless doubts repress our zeal; for, after all that we can do, we may rest assured, that our feeble

SERMON IX.

feeble efforts will never accelerate what the wifdom of God hath chofen to delay, and that the " fulnefs of the Gentiles will not come in" till the hour arrives, which God hath appointed from all eternity.

To his chofen people, to thofe who were under the protection of his peculiar providence, and of whom it was faid, that " to them falvation belonged ;" to this favoured race, God hath promifed, if we interpret aright the oracles of his word, that the hour fhall come, when " their eyes fhall be opened, and their hearts no longer hardened," and they fhall fee and confefs, that the Mefliah, whom their fathers crucified, and whom they ftill fo obftinately reject, is very Chrift and God."

" The children of Ifrael," fays Hofea, " fhall abide many days without a king, and without a prince, and without a facrifice, and without an image, and without an ephod, and without teraphim : afterward fhall the children of Ifrael return, and feek the Lord their God, and David their King; and fhall fear the Lord and his goodnefs
in

in the latter days [m];" and " it fhall come to pafs," fays Zechariah, " in that day, that I will feek to deftroy all the nations that come againft Jerufalem; and I will pour upon the houfe of David, and upon the inhabitants of Jerufalem, the fpirit of grace and of fupplications; and they fhall look upon him whom they have pierced, and they fhall mourn for him, as one mourneth for his only fon [n]." Thefe are two out of many prophecies, which point to the fame great event; but thefe are two of the moft remarkable, and they cannot be thought to allude to any event, or to any fituation of the Jewifh nation, prior to the crucifixion of our bleffed Redeemer. Upon all thefe prophecies of the Old Teftament, the holy Apoftle of the Gentiles is the beft commentator; he warns his converts, not to triumph and infult over the Jews, as if they were the outcafts of God, and aliens from his favour, for " blindnefs has happened," it is true, fays he " unto Ifrael; but it has happened only in part—it will ceafe when the fulnefs of the Gentiles fhall be come in, and then all Ifrael fhall be faved [o]."

[m] Hof. iii. 4, 5.   [n] Zeck. xii. 9, 10.   [o] Rom. xi. 25.

In what way conviction will operate at laft upon the mind of the Jew; whether he will yield his affent to the arguments of Chriftian writers, or whether the irrefiftible grace of God will withdraw the mift from his eyes, it is not poffible for us to determine. However this may be, it is enough for us to know, that he will be at length convinced; and we muft wait in filent awe, and with full and certain confidence, that all the deftinations of Divine wifdom, as they have been announced to us by the voice of Prophecy, will receive their full accomplifhment.

Chriftians meanwhile will be wanting to their duty, if they do not perfevere in their endeavours to convert that miftaken people to the true faith; if they do not lay before them the evidence which they poffefs in every poffible fhape, and try, by every argument, to overcome their rooted prepoffeffions. Chriftians will do well alfo to remember the injunction of the Apoftle; " Boaft not thyfelf againft the natural branches; be not high minded, but fear: for if God fpared not the natural branches, take heed, left he alfo

SERMON IX. 273

also spare not thee [q]." Our humble efforts, and our discreet endeavours, to forward the great cause of truth will receive, we may be assured, the gracious assistance of God; and to an attentive observer it must be evident, that his providence is continually opening the way for the general diffusion of the Gospel: for what other reason can we suppose, that the powers of Christendom were permitted to extend their empire to the Western world? and why else is the adventurous spirit of modern navigators so frequently rewarded by the discovery of new countries, and untried channels of communication between the various inhabitants of the globe? The wish to instruct then should keep pace with the power and the means of instruction; and it should be the first and greatest duty of Christian countries, to impart to others the blessings of civilization, which they have long enjoyed themselves; to call the ignorant barbarian from the pursuit of his scanty and precarious subsistence, to the enjoyment of the comforts, the conveniencies, and the elegancies of social life, and to give him the

[q] Rom. ii. 12. 21.

T   leisure

leisure and the opportunity to prepare his mind for the reception of those sacred truths, which are to connect us all in the unity of spirit, and in the bond of peace. The preparation of causes, it is true, may be distant; but when God himself has vouchsafed to announce his design, we cannot err in tracing them ultimately to that design; and surely in the successful cultivation of science, in the correction of flagrant errors, both in doctrine and in practice, in the enlarged and liberal intercourse between remote countries, and the invention of that art, which facilitates the diffusion of knowledge, we may discern the hand, that is imperceptibly guiding us to the great and final change in the religious state of mankind.

Perhaps too amongst the causes which seem likely to promote and extend the knowledge of Christ; to the love of *true* science, I may be permitted to add, the hatred and contempt, which we now entertain of those false and pernicious tenets, which chimerical theorists have long been attempting to force upon us.

Blessed

SERMON IX.

Blessed be God, that odious Philosophy, which was diffusing its baneful poison through every country of Christendom, hath lost the attractions which it once possessed. It has been tried, and we know it by its fruits; and it is to be hoped, that our ears will no more be insulted by fulsome panegyrics upon uncivilized ignorance; we shall not again be told, that a state of nature is preferable to a state of civilization; that a savage in the desert is a better, wiser, and happier being, than an educated Christian; and that if a man be moral, it matters little what God he adores, or whether he be a disciple of Jesus Christ, of Moses, or of Mahomet.

While the operation of moral causes is thus silently going on, under the control of Providence, the partial sufferings, the misfortunes, and the deprivations, which afflict the visible Church of Christ, ought not to depress the hope of the believer, or raise the wanton triumph of the infidel, because it is strictly conformable to the general tenor of the Divine government, from the evil which prevails in the world, from the fierce conflict of human paffions, and the oppofition of human interefts, ultimately to produce that good, which the Divine nature requires.

Sorrow, perfecution, and martyrdom, are the trials of the faithful fervant of God, and " for him that overcometh there is referved a crown of immortal glory." To the Chriftian Church, the Holy Spirit hath promifed, after perfecution, and diftrefs, and apoftafy, a long period of retribution and reft upon earth, " when the power of the evil one fhall be overthrown, and the Saints of the Moft High fhall reign." " Of the times, or the feafons, no man knoweth; the Father hath put them into his own power [r]."

Let the Chriftian wait then for " the defire of all nations [s]," as the devout Ifraelite of old did for the " confolation of Ifrael [t];" let him wait in full affurance, that " the myftery of God fhall be finifhed, as he hath declared to his fervants the Prophets [u]," and that " all the kingdoms of the

[r] Acts i. 7.
[t] Luke ii. 25.
[s] Hagg. ii. 7.
[u] Rev. x. 7.

earth

earth will become the kingdom of God, and his Chrift [x];" and, in the mean time, let him recollect, that when the fulnefs of that glorious kingdom is come, happy will that man be, who by the purity of his life, the energy of his precepts, or the prevailing influence of his example, hath contributed in any degree to accelerate its approach.

[x] Rev. xi. 15.

FINIS.

ERRATA.

Pag. 58. l. 2. read *sureſt*
To note q, p. 72. add *Hiſt.* v. 5.
Pag. 74. l. 18. dele *fomenting*
    133. l. 4. read *their*
    135. l. 20. read *who*
    146. l. 9. read *revived*
    160. l. 20. read *ſolicit*
    —— l. 21. read *triumphant*
    215. l. 5. read *yoke*
    222. l. 24. read *of worſhip*
    226. note d, read *See Joſeph. Antiqq.*
       lib. xi. c. 13.

www.ingramcontent.com/pod-product-compliance
Lightning Source LLC
Chambersburg PA
CBHW032100220426
43664CB00008B/1085